Life in the United Kingdom
Official Practice Questions
and Answers

a Williams Lea company

Published by TSO (The Stationery Office), part of Williams Lea, and available from:

Online
www.tsoshop.co.uk

Mail, Telephone, Fax & E-mail
TSO
PO Box 29, Norwich, NR3 1GN
Telephone orders/General enquiries: 0333 202 5070
Fax orders: 0333 202 5080
E-mail: customer.services@tso.co.uk
Textphone 0333 202 5077

TSO@Blackwell and other Accredited Agents

Contents

*This publication has been approved
by the Home Office.*

*TSO would like to thank Michael Mitchell who authored the
first edition of this publication.*

Introduction

The Life in the UK test

If you have decided that you would like to live in the UK permanently, or apply to become a British citizen, then you will need to pass the Life in the UK test.

The Life in the UK test is based on the content of the main Home Office publication, *Life in the United Kingdom: A Guide for New Residents*, published by The Stationery Office (TSO).

Preparing for your test

This book provides you with official practice questions to help you to answer the questions correctly in the Life in the UK test. So as soon as you have studied the main Home Office publication, you can start testing your knowledge. There are 408 questions in total in this book, arranged in 17 tests, each of 24 questions. Answers and helpful page references to the main Home Office publication are given at the end of each test, enabling you to see which pages you need to read again in the event of a wrong answer.

These practice questions are not the actual questions that you will get in the Life in the UK test, but by answering them correctly you can find out whether you are ready to take the test.

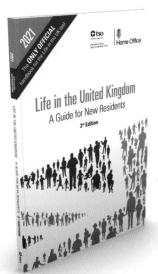

Before you take the test, you should aim to complete all the practice questions in this book. Complete one test at a time, and time yourself, allowing no more than 45 minutes per test. Note which questions you get wrong, and make sure you re-read the relevant pages in the main publication to ensure that your knowledge is sound.

When you go to the test centre to take the test, you can do a practice test of four questions before you start the actual test. You will have four minutes to do this practice test and you are allowed to take it twice before starting.

About the test

The Life in the UK test consists of 24 questions about important aspects of life in the UK today. You will take your test on a computer, and have 45 minutes to complete all the questions. In order to pass the test, you have to answer 18 questions correctly. The questions are based on ALL parts of *Life in the United Kingdom: A Guide for New Residents.*

You can only take your test at a registered and approved test centre, and you can only book your test online at www.lifeintheuktest.gov.uk

Types of question you will be asked

There are four types of question in the test. Each practice test in this book contains examples of each of these types of question, presented in random order.

The first type of question involves **selecting one correct answer from four options**. Here is an example of this type of question.

Which is the most popular sport in the UK?

☐ **A** Football

☐ **B** Rugby

☐ **C** Golf

☐ **D** Tennis

(The correct answer is A.)

The second type of question involves **deciding whether a statement is true or false**. Here is an example of this second type of question.

Is the statement below ☐ TRUE or ☐ FALSE?

The daffodil is the national flower of Wales.

(The correct answer is TRUE.)

The third type of question involves **selecting the statement which you think is correct** from a choice of two statements. Here is an example of this third type of question.

Which of the following statements is correct?

☐ **A** Shakespeare wrote 'To be or not to be'.

☐ **B** Shakespeare wrote 'We shall fight on the beaches'.

(The correct answer is A.)

The final type of question involves **selecting two correct answers from four options**. You need to select both correct answers to get a point on this type of question. Here is an example of this fourth type of question.

Which TWO political parties formed the coalition government in 2010?

☐ **A**   Conservatives

☐ **B**   Labour

☐ **C**   Communists

☐ **D**   Liberal Democrats

(The correct answer is A and D.)

Where can I find out more information about the test?

You can find more information on the Official Life in the UK website. The site features the Official Life in the UK e-learning, as well as other important resources such as the Life in the United Kingdom Official Study Guide. Visit www.officiallifeintheuk.co.uk for details.

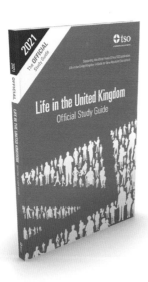

Practice Test 1

Question 1   Is the statement below ☐ TRUE or ☐ FALSE?

Charles Dickens was famous for writing musicals.

Question 2   Is the statement below ☐ TRUE or ☐ FALSE?

A General Election occurs every eight years.

Question 3   Is the statement below ☐ TRUE or ☐ FALSE?

In the UK you are expected to respect the rights of others to have their own opinions.

Question 4   Is the statement below ☐ TRUE or ☐ FALSE?

On the 1st of April, people in the UK play jokes on each other until midday.

Question 5   Which of the following statements is correct?

☐ **A** Shakespeare wrote 'To be or not to be'.

☐ **B** Shakespeare wrote 'We shall fight on the beaches'.

Question 6   How can you reduce your carbon footprint?

☐ **A** Shop locally for products

☐ **B** Buy duty-free products when you're abroad

☐ **C** Do all your shopping online

☐ **D** Drive to the supermarket

Question 7   Which of the following statements is correct?

☐ **A** The civil service largely consists of political appointees.

☐ **B** The civil service is politically neutral.

Question 8   Which TWO are Protestant Christian groups in the UK?

☐ **A**   Methodists and Roman Catholics

☐ **B**   Baptists and Hindus

☐ **C**   Baptists and Methodists

☐ **D**   Roman Catholics and Sikhs

Question 9   What is the role of a jury at a court trial?

☐ **A**   To decide whether evidence should be allowed to be heard

☐ **B**   To decide the sentence that the accused should be given

☐ **C**   To decide who the judge should be

☐ **D**   To decide a verdict based on what they have heard.

Question 10   Which form of comedy became famous in the 19th century?

☐ **A**   Sitcoms

☐ **B**   Satirical magazines

☐ **C**   Progressive comedy

☐ **D**   Court jesters

Question 11   During which period did John Barbour and other poets begin to write poetry in the Scots language?

☐ **A**   The 19th century

☐ **B**   The 20th century

☐ **C**   The Middle Ages

☐ **D**   The Bronze Age

Question 12 What are *Beowulf, The Tyger* and *She Walks in Beauty?*

☐ **A** Plays
☐ **B** Films
☐ **C** Poems
☐ **D** Novels

Question 13 What is a jury made up of?

☐ **A** People working in high-powered jobs
☐ **B** People randomly chosen from the electoral register
☐ **C** People who are members of political parties
☐ **D** People who have submitted an application form and been accepted

Question 14 Which TWO fought in wars against Napoleon?

☐ **A** Winston Churchill and the Duke of Wellington
☐ **B** Margaret Thatcher and the Duke of Wellington
☐ **C** Margaret Thatcher and Admiral Nelson
☐ **D** Admiral Nelson and the Duke of Wellington

Question 15 After slavery was abolished in the British Empire, more than 2 million migrants came from which TWO countries to replace the freed slaves?

☐ **A** India and China
☐ **B** Russia and China
☐ **C** India and Australia
☐ **D** Russia and Australia

Question 16 Which of the following groups of adults is NOT eligible to vote in all UK elections?

☐ **A** Citizens of the USA

☐ **B** Adult citizens of the UK

☐ **C** Citizens of the Commonwealth who are resident in the UK

☐ **D** Citizens of Ireland who are resident in the UK

Question 17 Which of the following statements is correct?

☐ **A** Big Ben is a mountain in eastern England.

☐ **B** Big Ben is the nickname for the great bell of the clock at the Houses of Parliament.

Question 18 Bobby Moore is famous for his achievements in which sport?

☐ **A** Football

☐ **B** Rugby union

☐ **C** Horse racing

☐ **D** Motor racing

Question 19 Is the statement below ☐ TRUE or ☐ FALSE?

If you are a Commonwealth citizen living in the UK, you can vote in all public elections.

Question 20 Which TWO of the following were important 20th-century inventors?

☐ **A** Tim Berners-Lee and Isambard Kingdom Brunel

☐ **B** Alan Turing and Tim Berners-Lee

☐ **C** George Stephenson and Isambard Kingdom Brunel

☐ **D** Alan Turing and George Stephenson

Question 21 Which of the following statements is correct?

☐ **A** When you apply to become a UK citizen or permanent resident, you can choose which laws and responsibilities you want to accept.

☐ **B** When you apply to become a UK citizen or permanent resident, you will be agreeing to respect the laws, values and traditions of the UK.

Question 22 Which TWO are plays by William Shakespeare?

☐ **A** *A Midsummer Night's Dream*, and *Oliver Twist*

☐ **B** *Romeo and Juliet*, and *Oliver Twist*

☐ **C** *A Midsummer Night's Dream*, and *Romeo and Juliet*

☐ **D** *Pride and Prejudice*, and *Romeo and Juliet*

Question 23 Which TWO commemorations or celebrations are held in November each year?

☐ **A** Remembrance Day and Bonfire Night

☐ **B** Father's Day and Valentine's Day

☐ **C** Valentine's Day and Remembrance Day

☐ **D** Valentine's Day and Bonfire Night

Question 24 Is the statement below ☐ TRUE or ☐ FALSE?

All young people are sent a National Insurance number just before their 16th birthday.

Answers to Practice Test 1

Question number	Answer	Explanation	Handbook chapter	Handbook page reference
1	FALSE	Charles Dickens wrote a number of famous novels, including *Oliver Twist* and *Great Expectations*.	A modern, thriving society	Page 98
2	FALSE	A General Election is held at least every five years.	The UK government, the law and your role	Page 125
3	TRUE	There are responsibilities and freedoms which are shared by all those living in the UK. These include respecting the rights of others, including their right to their own opinions.	The values and principle of the UK	Page 8
4	TRUE	April Fool's Day, 1 April, is a day when people play jokes on each other until midday. The television and newspapers often have stories that are April Fool jokes.	A modern, thriving society	Page 82
5	A	'To be or not to be' is a quotation from *Hamlet*, written by William Shakespeare.	A long and illustrious history	Page 30
6	A	A good way to support your local community is to shop for products locally where you can. This will help businesses and farmers in your area and in Britain. It will also reduce your carbon footprint, because the products you buy will not have had to travel as far.	The UK government, the law and your role	Page 160
7	B	Civil servants support the government in developing and implementing its policies. They are chosen on merit and are politically neutral – they are not political appointees.	The UK government, the law and your role	Page 128

Question number	Answer	Explanation	Handbook chapter	Handbook page reference
8	C	Baptists and Methodists are Protestant Christian groups. Other Protestant groups in the UK include the Church of England, the Church of Scotland, Presbyterians and Quakers.	A modern, thriving society	Page 77
9	D	A jury has to listen to the evidence presented at the trial and then decide a verdict of 'guilty' or 'not guilty' based on what they have heard. In Scotland, a third verdict of 'not proven' is also possible. If the jury finds a defendant guilty, the judge decides on the penalty.	The UK government, the law and your role	Page 146
10	B	The traditions of comedy and satire, and the ability to laugh at ourselves, are an important part of the UK character. In the 19th century, satirical magazines began to be published. The most famous was *Punch*, which was published for the first time in the 1840s.	A modern, thriving society	Page 104
11	C	In the Middle Ages a number of poets began to write in the Scots language. One example is John Barbour, who wrote *The Bruce* about the Battle of Bannockburn.	A long and illustrious history	Page 24
12	C	*Beowulf* is an Anglo-Saxon poem, *The Tyger* is a poem by William Blake, and *She Walks in Beauty* is a poem by Lord Byron.	A modern, thriving society	Pages 99–100
13	B	A jury is made up of members of the public chosen at random from the local electoral register.	The UK government, the law and your role	Page 134

Question number	Answer	Explanation	Handbook chapter	Handbook page reference
14	D	Admiral Nelson commanded the British fleet at the Battle of Trafalgar in 1805. He died during the battle. The Duke of Wellington defeated Napoleon at the Battle of Waterloo in 1815.	A long and illustrious history	Page 44
15	A	After 1833, 2 million Indian and Chinese workers were employed to replace the freed slaves.	A long and illustrious history	Page 43
16	A	Adult citizens of the UK, and citizens of the Commonwealth and Ireland who are resident in the UK, can vote in all public elections.	The UK government, the law and your role	Page 133
17	B	Big Ben is the nickname for the great bell of the clock at the Houses of Parliament in London. Many people call the clock Big Ben as well.	A modern, thriving society	Page 108
18	A	Bobby Moore captained the England football team that won the World Cup in 1966.	A modern, thriving society	Page 85
19	TRUE	Adult citizens of the UK, and citizens of the Commonwealth and Ireland who are resident in the UK, can vote in all public elections.	The UK government, the law and your role	Page 133

Question number	Answer	Explanation	Handbook chapter	Handbook page reference
20	B	Alan Turing (1912–54) invented a theoretical mathematical device called a Turing Machine that led to the development of the modern-day computer. Tim Berners-Lee (1955–) invented the World Wide Web.	A long and illustrious history	Pages 64–5
21	B	Applying to become a permanent resident or citizen of the UK is an important decision and commitment. You will be agreeing to accept the responsibilities which go with permanent residence and to respect the laws, values and traditions of the UK.	The values and principles of the UK	Page 7
22	C	Among the many plays that Shakespeare wrote are *A Midsummer Night's Dream* and *Romeo and Juliet*.	A long and illustrious history	Page 30
23	A	Bonfire Night, 5 November, is an occasion when people in Great Britain set off fireworks at home or in special displays. Remembrance Day, 11 November, commemorates those who died fighting for the UK and its allies.	A modern, thriving society	Page 83
24	TRUE	All young people in the UK are sent a National Insurance number just before their 16th birthday. It makes sure that the National Insurance Contributions and tax you pay are properly recorded against your name.	The UK government, the law and your role	Page 152

Practice Test 2

Question 1   Is the statement below ☐ TRUE or ☐ FALSE?

The Civil War between Charles I and Parliament in the mid-17th century led to Oliver Cromwell becoming king of England.

Question 2   Which event is remembered on 5 November each year?

☐ **A** The end of the Second World War

☐ **B** The Queen's birthday

☐ **C** A plan to blow up the Houses of Parliament in 1605

☐ **D** The defeat of the Spanish Armada in 1588

Question 3   When is Boxing Day?

☐ **A** The day after Easter

☐ **B** The day after Christmas Day

☐ **C** The last Monday in August

☐ **D** The first day in May

Question 4   Which group of refugees settled in England between 1680 and 1720?

☐ **A** Welsh

☐ **B** Germans

☐ **C** Bretons

☐ **D** Huguenots

Question 5   Is the statement below ☐ TRUE or ☐ FALSE?

'We shall fight on the beaches' is a famous quote from a speech by Queen Elizabeth I about the Spanish Armada.

Question 6   Is the statement below ☐ TRUE or ☐ FALSE?

Britain has never been at war with France.

Question 7   Which TWO are famous British fashion designers?

☐ **A** Capability Brown and Edwin Lutyens

☐ **B** Mary Quant and Capability Brown

☐ **C** Mary Quant and Vivienne Westwood

☐ **D** Capability Brown and Vivienne Westwood

Question 8   Which TWO services are funded by National Insurance Contributions?

☐ **A** State retirement pension and National Health Service (NHS)

☐ **B** Supermarket home deliveries and National Health Service (NHS)

☐ **C** Local taxi services and state retirement pension

☐ **D** State retirement pension and supermarket home deliveries

Question 9   Is the statement below ☐ TRUE or ☐ FALSE?

Cardiff, Swansea and Newport are cities in England.

Question 10 Which TWO developments were features of the Industrial Revolution?

☐ **A** Machinery and steam power

☐ **B** Changes in the law and steam power

☐ **C** Machinery and medical advances

☐ **D** Medical advances and changes in the law

Question 11   Who has to pay National Insurance Contributions?

- ☐ **A**   Almost everybody in the UK who is in paid work
- ☐ **B**   Only people who work full-time
- ☐ **C**   Only those aged 50 and below
- ☐ **D**   Only single people with no dependants

Question 12   Is the statement below ☐ TRUE or ☐ FALSE?

A husband who forces his wife to have sex can be charged with rape.

Question 13   Is the statement below ☐ TRUE or ☐ FALSE?

All people in the UK are expected to help the police prevent and detect crimes whenever they can.

Question 14   Is the statement below ☐ TRUE or ☐ FALSE?

In 1805, at the Battle of Trafalgar, Admiral Nelson defeated the German fleet.

Question 15   Is the statement below ☐ TRUE or ☐ FALSE?

Anybody can be asked to serve on a jury, no matter how old they are.

Question 16   Is the statement below ☐ TRUE or ☐ FALSE?

There is no place in British society for extremism or intolerance.

Question 17   Which of the following statements is correct?

- ☐ **A**   By 1400 the preferred language of the royal court was French.
- ☐ **B**   By 1400 the preferred language of the royal court was English.

Question 18 Which TWO of these novels are by Charles Dickens?

☐ **A** *Harry Potter* and *Great Expectations*

☐ **B** *Great Expectations* and *Oliver Twist*

☐ **C** *Harry Potter*, and *Pride and Prejudice*

☐ **D** *Pride and Prejudice*, and *Oliver Twist*

Question 19 At which festival are mince pies traditionally eaten?

☐ **A** Easter

☐ **B** Diwali

☐ **C** Christmas

☐ **D** Vaisakhi

Question 20 Is the statement below ☐ TRUE or ☐ FALSE?

During the 18th century, new ideas about politics, philosophy and science were developed. This period is often called 'the Enlightenment'.

Question 21 What is the youngest age at which you can be asked to serve on a jury?

☐ **A** 22

☐ **B** 18

☐ **C** 16

☐ **D** 30

Question 22 Is the statement below ☐ TRUE or ☐ FALSE?

An example of a civil law case is when you have purchased a faulty item and made a legal complaint.

Question 23 Which TWO of the following are famous British artists?

☐ **A** David Hockney and Henry Moore

☐ **B** David Hockney and Sir Edward Elgar

☐ **C** Sir Edward Elgar and Henry Moore

☐ **D** Sir Andy Murray and Sir Edward Elgar

Question 24 Which TWO of the following countries are members of the Commonwealth?

☐ **A** USA and Australia

☐ **B** Australia and Canada

☐ **C** Canada and Russia

☐ **D** Australia and Russia

Answers to Practice Test 2

Question number	Answer	Explanation	Handbook chapter	Handbook page reference
1	FALSE	At the end of the Civil War, England became a republic and Oliver Cromwell was given the title of Lord Protector.	A long and illustrious history	Page 34
2	C	Bonfire Night, 5 November, is an occasion when people in Great Britain set off fireworks at home or in special displays. The origin of this celebration was an event in 1605, when a group of Catholics led by Guy Fawkes failed in their plan to kill the Protestant king with a bomb in the Houses of Parliament.	A modern, thriving society	Page 83
3	B	Boxing Day is the day after Christmas Day and is a public holiday.	A modern, thriving society	Page 80
4	D	Between 1680 and 1720 many refugees called Huguenots came from France. They were Protestants and had been persecuted for their religion.	A long and illustrious history	Page 38
5	FALSE	'We shall fight on the beaches' is a quote from a speech by Winston Churchill, the Prime Minister, after the evacuation of Dunkirk in 1940.	A long and illustrious history	Page 57
6	FALSE	Britain fought a number of wars with France during the Middle Ages and later.	A long and illustrious history	Page 21
7	C	Britain has produced many great designers. Leading fashion designers of recent years include Mary Quant, Alexander McQueen and Vivienne Westwood.	A modern, thriving society	Page 97

Question number	Answer	Explanation	Handbook chapter	Handbook page reference
8	A	The money raised from National Insurance Contributions is used to pay for state benefits and services such as the state retirement pension and the National Health Service (NHS).	The UK government, the law and your role	Page 151
9	FALSE	Cardiff, Swansea and Newport are all cities in Wales.	A modern, thriving society	Page 72
10	A	Britain was the first country to industrialise on a large scale. This happened because of the development of machinery and the use of steam power.	A long and illustrious history	Page 40
11	A	Almost everybody in the UK who is in paid work, including self-employed people, must pay National Insurance Contributions. The money raised is used to pay for state benefits and services such as the state retirement pension and the National Health Service (NHS).	The UK government, the law and your role	Page 151
12	TRUE	Any man who forces a woman to have sex, including a woman's husband, can be charged with rape.	The UK government, the law and your role	Page 149
13	TRUE	All people in the UK are expected to help the police prevent and detect crimes whenever they can.	The UK government, the law and your role	Page 143
14	FALSE	Britain's navy fought against combined French and Spanish fleets, winning the Battle of Trafalgar in 1805. Admiral Nelson was in charge of the British fleet at Trafalgar and was killed in the battle.	A long and illustrious history	Page 44

Question number	Answer	Explanation	Handbook chapter	Handbook page reference
15	FALSE	Anyone who is on the electoral register and is aged 18–70 (18–75 in England and Wales) can be asked to serve on a jury.	The UK government, the law and your role	Page 155
16	TRUE	British society is founded on fundamental values and principles which all those living in the UK respect and support. There is no place for extremism or intolerance.	The values and principles of the UK	Page 7
17	B	By 1400 the preferred language of the royal court was English, which was also the language of official documents.	A long and illustrious history	Page 23
18	B	Charles Dickens wrote a number of very famous novels, including *Oliver Twist* and *Great Expectations*.	A modern, thriving society	Page 98
19	C	Christmas is celebrated in a traditional way. People usually spend the day at home and eat a special meal, which often includes roast turkey, Christmas pudding and mince pies.	A modern, thriving society	Page 79
20	TRUE	During the 18th century, new ideas about politics, philosophy and science were developed. This period is often called 'the Enlightenment'. One of the most important principles of the Enlightenment was that everyone should have the right to their own political and religious beliefs and that the state should not try to dictate to them.	A long and illustrious history	Page 40
21	B	Anyone who is on the electoral register and is aged 18–70 (18–75 in England and Wales) can be asked to serve on a jury.	The UK government, the law and your role	Page 155

Question number	Answer	Explanation	Handbook chapter	Handbook page reference
22	TRUE	Civil law is used to settle disputes between individuals or groups.	The UK government, the law and your role	Page 140
23	A	David Hockney was an important contributor to the 'pop art' movement of the 1960s. Henry Moore is best known for his large bronze abstract sculptures.	A modern, thriving society	Pages 94–5
24	B	Australia and Canada are members of the Commonwealth. The Queen is the ceremonial head of the Commonwealth, which currently has 54 member states.	The UK government, the law and your role	Page 137

Practice Test 3

Question 1   Which of the following statements is correct?

☐ **A** Carrying a weapon is an example of a criminal offence.

☐ **B** Being in debt is an example of a criminal offence.

Question 2   Which TWO developments are associated with the 'Swinging Sixties'?

☐ **A** Reform of abortion law and introduction of decimal currency

☐ **B** Reform of children's rights law and introduction of decimal currency

☐ **C** Reform of children's rights law and reform of divorce law

☐ **D** Reform of abortion law and reform of divorce law

Question 3   Which TWO religions celebrate Diwali?

☐ **A** Hindus and Christians

☐ **B** Hindus and Sikhs

☐ **C** Christians and Sikhs

☐ **D** Buddhists and Christians

Question 4   During the 'Great Depression' of the 1930s, which TWO major new industries developed?

☐ **A** Automobiles and aviation

☐ **B** Ship building and coal mining

☐ **C** Ship building and aviation

☐ **D** Coal mining and automobiles

Question 5   Is the statement below ☐ TRUE or ☐ FALSE?

Dundee and Aberdeen are cities in Northern Ireland.

Question 6   Which TWO are examples of civil law?

☐ **A** Housing law and employment law

☐ **B** Drugs law and racial crime law

☐ **C** Employment law and drugs law

☐ **D** Housing law and racial crime law

Question 7   Which TWO of the following are Christian festivals celebrated in the UK?

☐ **A** Halloween and New Year

☐ **B** Easter and Christmas

☐ **C** Christmas and New Year

☐ **D** Easter and Halloween

Question 8   Which TWO of the following wars were English kings involved in during the Middle Ages?

☐ **A** The Crusades and the First World War

☐ **B** The Crimean War and the Crusades

☐ **C** The Crimean War and the Hundred Years War

☐ **D** The Crusades and the Hundred Years War

Question 9   Is the statement below ☐ TRUE or ☐ FALSE?

The Channel Islands are a part of the UK.

Question 10 What is a fundamental principle of British life?

☐ **A** Relaxed work ethic

☐ **B** Democracy

☐ **C** Extremism

☐ **D** Disrespect for the law

Question 11 Which of the following statements is correct?

☐ **A** Civil servants are politically neutral.

☐ **B** Civil servants have to be politically aligned to the elected government.

Question 12 Is the statement below ☐ TRUE or ☐ FALSE?

During the Victorian period the British Empire became the largest empire the world has ever seen.

Question 13 Which of the following statements is correct?

☐ **A** Florence Nightingale is associated with policing.

☐ **B** Florence Nightingale is associated with nursing.

Question 14 Which TWO of the following are UK landmarks?

☐ **A** Edinburgh Castle and the London Eye

☐ **B** The Eisteddfod and the National Trust

☐ **C** The National Trust and the London Eye

☐ **D** The National Trust and Edinburgh Castle

Question 15 Dylan Thomas was a famous writer and poet from which country?

- ☐ **A** England
- ☐ **B** Scotland
- ☐ **C** Wales
- ☐ **D** Northern Ireland

Question 16 Which of the following statements is correct?

- ☐ **A** County Courts deal with criminal cases.
- ☐ **B** County Courts deal with civil disputes.

Question 17 Which TWO of the following are famous Paralympians?

- ☐ **A** Ellie Simmonds and Baroness Tanni Grey-Thompson
- ☐ **B** Ellie Simmonds and Dame Ellen MacArthur
- ☐ **C** Dame Jessica Ennis-Hill and Baroness Tanni Grey-Thompson
- ☐ **D** Dame Jessica Ennis-Hill and Dame Ellen MacArthur

Question 18 Which of the following statements is correct?

- ☐ **A** Elizabeth I was not successful in balancing her wishes and views against those of the House of Lords and the House of Commons
- ☐ **B** Elizabeth I was successful in balancing her wishes and views against those of the House of Lords and the House of Commons

Question 19 Which court would you use to get back money that
was owed to you?

☐ **A** County Court

☐ **B** Magistrates' Court

☐ **C** Youth Court

☐ **D** Coroner's Court

Question 20 Which of the following statements is correct?

☐ **A** Every household with a device that can be used
to watch TV must have a television licence.

☐ **B** People who watch TV only on their computers
do not need to pay for a television licence.

Question 21 Is the statement below ☐ TRUE or ☐ FALSE?

*Emmeline Pankhurst is famous for her role in the campaign to
give women the vote in parliamentary elections in the UK.*

Question 22 Is the statement below ☐ TRUE or ☐ FALSE?

UK citizens must practise a Christian religion.

Question 23 Which of the following statements is correct?

☐ **A** People in paid work need to pay National
Insurance Contributions.

☐ **B** People in paid work do not need to pay National
Insurance Contributions.

Question 24 The Enlightenment led to major developments in which TWO areas?

☐ **A** Science and politics

☐ **B** History and theatre

☐ **C** Science and theatre

☐ **D** Politics and history

Answers to Practice Test 3

Question number	Answer	Explanation	Handbook chapter	Handbook page reference
1	A	Carrying a weapon is one example of a criminal offence. Crimes are usually investigated by the police and punished by the courts.	The UK government, the law and your role	Page 140
2	D	During the 1960s (a period known as the 'Swinging Sixties'), a number of social changes took place. Many social laws were liberalised, for example, in regard to abortion and divorce in England, Wales and Scotland.	A long and illustrious history	Page 63
3	B	Diwali is celebrated by Hindus and Sikhs. It celebrates the victory of good over evil and the gaining of knowledge.	A modern, thriving society	Page 81
4	A	During the Great Depression of the 1930s, many traditional heavy industries, such as shipbuilding, went into decline. However, new industries – such as aviation and the automobile industry – developed.	A long and illustrious history	Page 55
5	FALSE	Dundee and Aberdeen are cities in Scotland.	A modern, thriving society	Page 72
6	A	Civil law is used to settle disputes between individuals or groups. Examples of civil law include housing law, employment law, consumer rights and laws related to the recovery of debt.	The UK government, the law and your role	Page 141

Question number	Answer	Explanation	Handbook chapter	Handbook page reference
7	B	Easter and Christmas are two Christian festivals. Christmas celebrates the birth of Jesus Christ, and Easter marks his death on Good Friday and his rising from the dead on Easter Sunday.	A modern, thriving society	Pages 79–80
8	D	During the Middle Ages, the English kings fought a number of wars abroad. Many knights took part in the Crusades, in which European Christians fought for control of the Holy Land. English kings also fought a long war with France, called the Hundred Years War (even though it actually lasted 116 years).	A long and illustrious history	Page 21
9	FALSE	The Channel Islands are closely linked with the UK but are not part of it. They have their own governments and are called 'Crown dependencies'.	What is the UK?	Page 13
10	B	British society is founded on fundamental values and principles which all those living in the UK should respect and support. One of these principles is democracy.	The values and principles of the UK	Page 7
11	A	Civil servants are chosen on merit and are politically neutral – they are not political appointees.	The UK government, the law and your role	Page 128
12	TRUE	During the Victorian period, the British Empire grew to cover all of India, Australia and large parts of Africa. It became the largest empire the world has ever seen, with an estimated population of more than 400 million people.	A long and illustrious history	Page 47

Question number	Answer	Explanation	Handbook chapter	Handbook page reference
13	B	Florence Nightingale treated soldiers who were fighting in the Crimean War. She later established the Nightingale Training School for nurses at St Thomas' Hospital in London. She is often regarded as the founder of modern nursing.	A long and illustrious history	Page 49
14	A	Edinburgh Castle is a dominant feature of the skyline in Edinburgh, Scotland. The London Eye is situated on the southern bank of the River Thames. Both are UK landmarks.	A modern, thriving society	Pages 110 and 113
15	C	Dylan Thomas, who lived from 1914 until 1953, was a Welsh poet and writer. One of his most well-known works is *Under Milk Wood*.	A long and illustrious history	Page 62
16	B	County Courts deal with a wide range of civil disputes. These include people trying to get back money that is owed to them, cases involving personal injury, family matters, breaches of contract, and divorce.	The UK government, the law and your role	Page 146
17	A	Ellie Simmonds won gold medals for swimming at the 2008, 2012 and 2016 Paralympic Games. Baroness Tanni Grey-Thompson is an athlete who uses a wheelchair and won 16 Paralympic medals.	A modern, thriving society	Pages 85–6
18	B	Elizabeth was successful in balancing her wishes and views against those of the House of Lords and the House of Commons. Her successor James I and his son Charles I were less politically skilled.	A long and illustrious history	Page 32

Question number	Answer	Explanation	Handbook chapter	Handbook page reference
19	A	County Courts deal with a wide range of civil disputes. These include people trying to get back money that is owed to them.	The UK government, the law and your role	Page 146
20	A	Everyone in the UK with a TV, computer or other medium which can be used for watching TV must have a television licence. One licence covers all of the equipment in one home, except when people rent different rooms in a shared house and each has a separate tenancy agreement – those people must each buy a separate licence.	A modern, thriving society	Page 105
21	TRUE	Emmeline Pankhurst (1858–1928) helped found the Women's Social and Political Union (WSPU). This was the first group whose members were called 'suffragettes'. The group used civil disobedience as part of their protest to gain the vote for women.	A long and illustrious history	Page 51
22	FALSE	Everyone has the legal right to choose their religion, or to choose not to practise a religion.	A modern, thriving society	Page 76
23	A	Almost everybody in the UK who is in paid work must pay National Insurance Contributions. Employees have their National Insurance Contributions deducted from their pay by their employer.	The UK government, the law and your role	Page 151
24	A	During the 18th century, new ideas about politics, science and philosophy developed. This is often called 'the Enlightenment'.	A long and illustrious history	Page 40

Practice Test 4

Question 1   Which TWO of the following are examples of criminal law?

☐ **A** Disputes about faulty goods and discrimination in the workplace

☐ **B** Racial crime and discrimination in the workplace

☐ **C** Racial crime and disputes about faulty goods

☐ **D** Racial crime and selling tobacco to anyone under the age of 18

Question 2   Is the statement below ☐ TRUE or ☐ FALSE?

Britain and Germany developed Concorde, a supersonic passenger aircraft.

Question 3   Which of the following is dealt with under civil law?

☐ **A** Debt

☐ **B** Violent crime

☐ **C** Burglary

☐ **D** Disorderly behaviour

Question 4   Which TWO of the following are major horse-racing events in the UK?

☐ **A** The Open Championship and the Scottish Grand National

☐ **B** The Open Championship and the Six Nations Championship

☐ **C** Scottish Grand National and the Six Nations Championship

☐ **D** Scottish Grand National and Royal Ascot

Question 5   Is the statement below ☐ TRUE or ☐ FALSE?

*Florence Nightingale is famous for her work
on education in the 19th century.*

Question 6   Which of the following statements is correct?

☐ **A** There is no place in British society for extremism
or intolerance.

☐ **B** Britain encourages people to have extreme
views and to act upon them.

Question 7   What important event happened in England in 1066?

☐ **A** The Romans left England

☐ **B** The building of the Offa Dyke

☐ **C** The Norman Conquest

☐ **D** The Battle of Bannockburn

Question 8   Which event occurs each year on the third Sunday
in June?

☐ **A** Halloween

☐ **B** Father's Day

☐ **C** Boxing Day

☐ **D** Remembrance Day

Question 9   Which of the following statements is correct?

☐ **A** Donated blood is used by hospitals to help people
with a wide range of injuries and illnesses

☐ **B** Donated blood is not used by hospitals to help
people with a wide range of injuries and illnesses

Question 10 Which of the following was a well known author of children's books?

- ☐ **A** Roald Dahl
- ☐ **B** William Shakespeare
- ☐ **C** Graham Greene
- ☐ **D** Jane Austen

Question 11 What happened to Margaret Thatcher in 1979 to make her famous in UK history?

- ☐ **A** She took part in the Olympics.
- ☐ **B** She became a High Court judge.
- ☐ **C** She became the first woman Prime Minister.
- ☐ **D** She was made a general in the British army.

Question 12 Which of the following statements is correct?

- ☐ **A** Local elections are normally held in May.
- ☐ **B** Local elections are normally held in March.

Question 13 Which TWO of the following are major outdoor music festivals

- ☐ **A** Hogmanay and Glastonbury
- ☐ **B** Royal Ascot and the Isle of Wight Festival
- ☐ **C** Royal Ascot and Hogmanay
- ☐ **D** Isle of Wight Festival and Glastonbury

Question 14 After the Bill of Rights was passed in 1689, which TWO main political groups emerged?

☐ **A** Labour and Tories

☐ **B** Whigs and Tories

☐ **C** Whigs and Nationalists

☐ **D** Nationalists and Tories

Question 15 Is the statement below ☐ TRUE or ☐ FALSE?

Forcing another person to marry is a criminal offence in the UK.

Question 16 Which of the following statements is correct?

☐ **A** The first professional UK football clubs were formed in the late 19th century

☐ **B** The first professional UK football clubs were formed in 1066.

Question 17 Is the statement below ☐ TRUE or ☐ FALSE?

Getting to know your neighbours can help you to become part of the community.

Question 18 Which collection of poems was written by Geoffrey Chaucer?

☐ **A** The Westbury Tales

☐ **B** The Ambridge Tales

☐ **C** The London Tales

☐ **D** The Canterbury Tales

Question 19 Which is the most popular sport in the UK?

☐ **A** Football
☐ **B** Rugby
☐ **C** Golf
☐ **D** Tennis

Question 20 When a Member of Parliament (MP) dies or resigns, what is the election called that is held to replace them?

☐ **A** Re-selection
☐ **B** Selection
☐ **C** Hustings
☐ **D** By-election

Question 21 Which of the following statements is correct?

☐ **A** After the age of 70, drivers must renew their licence every three years.
☐ **B** After the age of 70, drivers must renew their licence every five years.

Question 22 In which country was the composer George Frederick Handel born?

☐ **A** Iceland
☐ **B** Russia
☐ **C** Japan
☐ **D** Germany

Question 23 Which of the following statements is correct?

☐ **A** George and Robert Stephenson were famous pioneers of railway engines.

☐ **B** George and Robert Stephenson were famous pioneers of agricultural changes.

Question 24 Which of the following is a famous garden in Scotland?

☐ **A** Hidcote

☐ **B** Inveraray Castle

☐ **C** Mount Stewart

☐ **D** Bodnant Garden

Answers to Practice Test 4

Question number	Answer	Explanation	Handbook chapter	Handbook page reference
1	D	Criminal law relates to crimes, which are usually investigated by the police or another authority such as a council, and which are punished by the courts. Examples of crimes include racial crime and selling tobacco to anyone under the age of 18.	The UK government, the law and your role	Page 140
2	FALSE	False - Britain and France developed Concorde, the supersonic passenger aircraft. It first flew in 1969 and began carrying passengers in 1976. Concorde was retired from service in 2003.	A long and illustrious history	Page 65
3	A	Debt is covered by civil law. People might be taken to court if they owe money to someone.	The UK government, the law and your role	Page 141
4	D	Famous horse-racing events include: Royal Ascot, a five-day race meeting in Berkshire attended by members of the Royal Family; and the Scottish Grand National at Ayr.	A modern, thriving society	Page 88
5	FALSE	Florence Nightingale (1820–1910) worked in military hospitals, treating soldiers who were fighting in the Crimean War. She and her fellow nurses improved the conditions in the hospital and reduced the mortality rate. She is often regarded as the founder of modern nursing.	A long and illustrious history	Page 49

Question number	Answer	Explanation	Handbook chapter	Handbook page reference
6	A	British society is founded on fundamental values and principles which all those living in the UK should respect and support. There is no place for extremism or intolerance.	The values and principles of the UK	Page 7
7	C	In 1066, William, the Duke of Normandy (in what is now northern France), defeated Harold, the Saxon king of England, at the Battle of Hastings. The Norman Conquest was the last successful foreign invasion of England and led to many changes in government and social structures in England.	A long and illustrious history	Page 19
8	B	Father's Day is the third Sunday in June. Children send cards or buy gifts for their fathers.	A modern, thriving society	Page 82
9	A	Donated blood is used by hospitals to help people with a wide range of injuries and illnesses. Giving blood only takes about an hour to do.	The UK government, the law and your role	Page 157
10	A	Roald Dahl was born in Wales to Norwegian parents. He is most well known for his children's books, although he also wrote for adults.	A long and illustrious history	Page 68
11	C	Following the Conservative victory in the General Election in 1979, Margaret Thatcher became the first woman Prime Minister of the UK. She was the longest-serving Prime Minister of the 20th century, remaining in office until 1990.	A long and illustrious history	Page 67

Question number	Answer	Explanation	Handbook chapter	Handbook page reference
12	A	For most local authorities, local elections for councillors are held in May every year.	The UK government, the law and your role	Page 129
13	D	Festival season takes place across the UK every summer, with major events in various locations. Famous festivals include Glastonbury, the Isle of Wight Festival and Creamfields.	A modern, thriving society	Page 92
14	B	From 1689 onwards there were two main groups in Parliament, known as the Whigs and the Tories.	A long and illustrious history	Page 37
15	TRUE	Forced marriage is where one or both parties do not or cannot give their consent to enter into the partnership. This is a criminal offence in the UK.	The UK government, the law and your role	Page 150
16	A	Football has a long history in the UK and the first professional football clubs were formed in the late 19th century.	A modern, thriving society	Page 87
17	TRUE	Getting to know your neighbours can help you to become part of the community and make friends. Your neighbours are also a good source of help.	The UK government, the law and your role	Page 154
18	D	Geoffrey Chaucer wrote a series of poems about a group of people going to Canterbury on a pilgrimage. This collection of poems is called *The Canterbury Tales*.	A long and illustrious history	Page 23
19	A	Football is the UK's most popular sport. It has a long history in the UK and the first professional football clubs were formed in the late 19th century.	A modern, thriving society	Page 87

Question number	Answer	Explanation	Handbook chapter	Handbook page reference
20	D	If a Member of Parliament (MP) dies or resigns, there will be a fresh election, called a by-election, in his or her constituency.	The UK government, the law and your role	Page 125
21	A	Drivers can use their driving licence until they are 70 years old. After that, the licence is valid for three years at a time.	The UK government, the law and your role	Page 152
22	D	George Frederick Handel was born in Germany in 1685. He spent many years in the UK and became a British citizen in 1727.	A modern, thriving society	Page 90
23	A	George and Robert Stephenson were famous pioneers of railway engines.	A long and illustrious history	Page 48
24	B	Inveraray Castle is a famous garden in Scotland.	A long and illustrious history	Page 101

Practice Test 5

Question 1 Is the statement below ☐ TRUE or ☐ FALSE?

If an accused person is aged 18 to 21, their case will be heard in a Youth Court.

Question 2 Which TWO of the following are fundamental principles of British life?

☐ **A** Only driving your car on weekdays and participation in community life

☐ **B** Participation in community life and tolerance of those with different faiths and beliefs

☐ **C** Only driving your car on weekdays and growing your own fruit and vegetables

☐ **D** Growing your own fruit and vegetables and tolerance of those with different faiths and beliefs

Question 3 What is the name of the Houses of Parliament's clock tower?

☐ **A** Big Ben Tower

☐ **B** Parliament Tower

☐ **C** House of Commons Tower

☐ **D** Elizabeth Tower

Question 4 Which of the following was a famous British inventor?

☐ **A** Dylan Thomas

☐ **B** Clement Atlee

☐ **C** Emmeline Pankhurst

☐ **D** Sir Peter Mansfield

Question 5   Which of the following statements is correct?

☐ **A** Jane Austen and Charles Dickens were famous novelists.

☐ **B** Jane Austen and Charles Dickens were famous painters.

Question 6   Which of the following is a traditional food associated with Scotland?

☐ **A** Roast beef

☐ **B** Ulster fry

☐ **C** Fish and chips

☐ **D** Haggis

Question 7   When is a by-election for a parliamentary seat held?

☐ **A** Half-way through a parliamentary term

☐ **B** Every two years

☐ **C** When a Member of Parliament (MP) dies or resigns

☐ **D** When the Prime Minister decides to call one

Question 8   Which of the following statements is correct?

☐ **A** Halloween is when lovers exchange cards and gifts.

☐ **B** Halloween has its roots in an ancient pagan festival marking the beginning of winter.

Question 9   Which of the following statements is correct?

☐ **A** In 1588 the English defeated the Spanish Armada.

☐ **B** In 1588 the English defeated German bomber planes.

Question 10 Which TWO actions can a judge take if a public body is not respecting someone's legal rights?

☐ **A** Order the body to pay compensation and close down the public body.

☐ **B** Place the body's members in prison and close down the public body.

☐ **C** Order the body to change its practices and order the body to pay compensation.

☐ **D** Place the body's members in prison and order the body to change its practices.

Question 11 Who invaded England in 1066?

☐ **A** Richard the Lionheart

☐ **B** King Canute

☐ **C** William, the Duke of Normandy

☐ **D** Harold of Wessex

Question 12 Which of the following statements is correct?

☐ **A** In a Crown Court case, the judge decides the penalty when someone is found guilty.

☐ **B** In a Crown Court case, the jury decides the penalty when someone is found guilty.

Question 13 Which of these events changed the powers of the king in 1215?

- ☐ **A** The Domesday Book
- ☐ **B** The Magna Carta
- ☐ **C** The Reform Act
- ☐ **D** The Black Death

Question 14 Which TWO are famous British composers?

- ☐ **A** Henry Purcell and Ralph Vaughan Williams
- ☐ **B** Johann Sebastian Bach and Henry Purcell
- ☐ **C** Claude Debussy and Henry Purcell
- ☐ **D** Claude Debussy and Johann Sebastian Bach

Question 15 If your car is more than three years old, how often will it need a Ministry of Transport (MOT) test?

- ☐ **A** Every three years
- ☐ **B** Every six months
- ☐ **C** Every 10 years
- ☐ **D** Every year

Question 16 In 1348 a third of the populations of England, Wales and Scotland died as a result of which plague?

- ☐ **A** The Blue Death
- ☐ **B** The White Death
- ☐ **C** The Green Death
- ☐ **D** The Black Death

Question 17 What type of church is the Church of Scotland?

☐ **A** Quaker

☐ **B** Roman Catholic

☐ **C** Presbyterian

☐ **D** Methodist

Question 18 Is the statement below ☐ TRUE or ☐ FALSE?

Participating in your community is a fundamental principle of British life.

Question 19 Which of the following statements is correct?

☐ **A** The Wars of the Roses were between the Houses of Lancaster and York.

☐ **B** The Wars of the Roses were between the Houses of Windsor and Tudor.

Question 20 What important change to our voting rights took place in 1969?

☐ **A** Women over 35 were given the vote.

☐ **B** Prisoners were given the vote.

☐ **C** The voting age was reduced to 18 for men and women.

☐ **D** Compulsory voting was introduced.

Question 21   In 1776, 13 British colonies declared their independence. In which part of the world were these colonies?

☐ **A** Australia

☐ **B** Canada

☐ **C** America

☐ **D** South Africa

Question 22   Which of the following statements is correct?

☐ **A** Lancelot 'Capability' Brown and Gertrude Jekyll were famous garden designers.

☐ **B** Lancelot 'Capability' Brown and Gertrude Jekyll were famous characters in a Sherlock Holmes story.

Question 23   Which TWO are famous horse-racing events?

☐ **A** The Cup Final and the Six Nations

☐ **B** The Grand National and Royal Ascot

☐ **C** Royal Ascot and the Six Nations

☐ **D** The Grand National and the Cup Final

Question 24   What is the minimum age you can drive a car or motor cycle in the UK?

☐ **A** 17

☐ **B** 21

☐ **C** 18

☐ **D** 25

Answers to Practice Test 5

Question number	Answer	Explanation	Handbook chapter	Handbook page reference
1	FALSE	If an accused person is aged 10 to 17, the case is normally held in a Youth Court.	The UK government, the law and your role	Page 146
2	B	British society is founded on fundamental values and principles which all those living in the UK should respect and support. These include participation in community life and tolerance of those with different faiths and beliefs.	The values and principles of the UK	Page 8
3	D	The clock tower is named 'Elizabeth Tower' in honour of Queen Elizabeth II's Diamond Jubilee in 2012.	A modern, thriving society	Page 108
4	D	Sir Peter Mansfield (1933–2017), a British scientist, is the co-inventor of the MRI (magnetic resonance imaging) scanner. This enables doctors and researchers to obtain exact and non-invasive images of human internal organs and has revolutionised diagnostic medicine.	A long and illustrious history	Page 65
5	A	Jane Austen and Charles Dickens were famous novelists. Jane Austen's books include *Pride and Prejudice*, and *Sense and Sensibility*. Charles Dickens's novels include *Oliver Twist* and *Great Expectations*.	A modern, thriving society	Page 98
6	D	Haggis is a traditional Scottish food. It is a sheep's stomach stuffed with offal, suet, onions and oatmeal.	A modern, thriving society	Page 102

Question number	Answer	Explanation	Handbook chapter	Handbook page reference
7	C	If an MP dies or resigns, there will be a fresh election, called a by-election, in his or her constituency.	The UK government, the law and your role	Page 125
8	B	Halloween is an ancient festival and has its roots in the pagan festival to mark the beginning of winter.	A modern, thriving society	Page 82
9	A	In 1588, the English defeated the Spanish Armada (a large fleet of ships), which had been sent by Spain to conquer England and restore Catholicism.	A long and illustrious history	Page 29
10	C	If judges find that a public body is not respecting someone's legal rights, they can order that body to change its practices and/or pay compensation.	The UK government, the law and your role	Page 144
11	C	In 1066, William, the Duke of Normandy, invaded England and defeated King Harold at the Battle of Hastings.	A long and illustrious history	Page 19
12	A	If the jury in a Crown Court case finds the defendant guilty, the judge decides on the penalty.	The UK government, the law and your role	Page 146
13	B	In 1215, King John was forced by his noblemen to agree to a number of demands. The result was a charter of rights called the Magna Carta (which means the Great Charter). The Magna Carta established the idea that even the king was subject to the law. It protected the rights of the nobility and restricted the king's power to collect taxes or to make or change laws.	A long and illustrious history	Page 22

Question number	Answer	Explanation	Handbook chapter	Handbook page reference
14	A	Henry Purcell wrote church music, opera and other pieces, and developed a British style distinct from that elsewhere in Europe. Ralph Vaughan Williams wrote music for orchestras and choirs. He was strongly influenced by traditional English folk music.	A modern, thriving society	Pages 90–1
15	D	If your car is over three years old, you must take it for a Ministry of Transport (MOT) test every year. It is an offence not to have an MOT certificate if your vehicle is more than three years old.	The UK government, the law and your role	Page 153
16	D	In 1348, a disease, probably a form of plague, came to Britain. This was known as the Black Death. One third of the population of England died and a similar proportion in Scotland and Wales. This was one of the worst disasters ever to strike Britain.	A long and illustrious history	Page 22
17	C	In Scotland, the national Church is the Church of Scotland, which is a Presbyterian Church.	A modern, thriving society	Page 77
18	TRUE	British society is founded on fundamental values and principles which all those living in the UK should respect and support. This includes participating in community life.	The values and principles of the UK	Page 8
19	A	In 1455, a civil war was begun to decide who should be king of England. It was fought between the supporters of two families: the House of Lancaster and the House of York. This war was called the Wars of the Roses, because the symbol of Lancaster was a red rose and the symbol of York was a white rose.	A long and illustrious history	Page 25

Question number	Answer	Explanation	Handbook chapter	Handbook page reference
20	C	In 1969, the voting age was reduced to 18 for men and women.	The UK government, the law and your role	Page 120
21	C	In 1776, 13 American colonies declared their independence, stating that people had a right to establish their own governments. The colonists eventually defeated the British army and Britain recognised the colonies' independence in 1783.	A long and illustrious history	Page 44
22	A	In the 18th century, Lancelot 'Capability' Brown designed the grounds around country houses so that the landscape appeared to be natural, with grass, trees and lakes. Later, Gertrude Jekyll often worked with Edwin Lutyens to design colourful gardens around the houses he designed.	A modern, thriving society	Page 97
23	B	Famous horse-racing events include: Royal Ascot, a five-day race meeting in Berkshire attended by members of the Royal Family; the Grand National at Aintree near Liverpool; and the Scottish Grand National at Ayr.	A modern, thriving society	Page 88
24	A	In the UK, you must be at least 17 years old to drive a car or motor cycle and you must have a driving licence to drive on public roads.	The UK government, the law and your role	Page 152

Practice Test 6

Question 1   How old do you need to be in order to stand for public office?

☐ **A** 16
☐ **B** 18
☐ **C** 20
☐ **D** 21

Question 2   What sort of cases do Crown Courts and Sheriff Courts deal with?

☐ **A** Small claims procedures
☐ **B** Youth cases
☐ **C** Minor criminal cases
☐ **D** Serious offences

Question 3   What is the minimum age at which you can legally buy alcohol in the UK?

☐ **A** 20
☐ **B** 21
☐ **C** 18
☐ **D** 19

Question 4   Which TWO famous London buildings are built in the 19th-century 'gothic' style?

☐ **A** The Houses of Parliament and Buckingham Palace
☐ **B** St Paul's Cathedral and St Pancras Station
☐ **C** St Paul's Cathedral and Buckingham Palace
☐ **D** The Houses of Parliament and St Pancras Station

Question 5   How many people serve on a jury in Scotland?

☐ **A** 8

☐ **B** 11

☐ **C** 15

☐ **D** 20

Question 6   Is the statement below ☐ TRUE or ☐ FALSE?

In 1588 the English defeated the Spanish Armada.

Question 7   Which TWO members of a family have a special day dedicated to them?

☐ **A** Uncles and aunts

☐ **B** Mothers and aunts

☐ **C** Fathers and aunts

☐ **D** Fathers and mothers

Question 8   How old do you have to be to go into a betting shop in the UK?

☐ **A** 21

☐ **B** 18

☐ **C** 25

☐ **D** 30

Question 9   Which of the following statements is correct?

☐ **A** In 1776, 13 American colonies declared their independence from Britain.

☐ **B** The American colonists were eventually defeated by the British.

Question 10 How old must you be to ride a moped in the UK?

- ☐ **A** 18
- ☐ **B** 25
- ☐ **C** 16
- ☐ **D** 21

Question 11 Which of the following statements is correct?

- ☐ **A** Gilbert and Sullivan were a comedy double act.
- ☐ **B** Gilbert and Sullivan wrote many comic operas.

Question 12 Is the following statement ☐ TRUE or ☐ FALSE?

British values and principles are based on history and traditions.

Question 13 Is the statement below ☐ TRUE or ☐ FALSE?

In 1833 the Emancipation Act abolished slavery throughout the British Empire.

Question 14 Which of these is the name of a novel by Jane Austen?

- ☐ **A** *Sense and Sensibility*
- ☐ **B** *Far from the Madding Crowd*
- ☐ **C** *Oliver Twist*
- ☐ **D** *Our Man in Havana*

Question 15 Which TWO things can you do to look after the environment?

- ☐ **A** Recycle your waste and never turn your lights off in your house.
- ☐ **B** Drive your car as much as possible and never turn the lights off in your house.
- ☐ **C** Recycle your waste and walk and use public transport to get around.
- ☐ **D** Drive your car as much as possible and recycle your waste.

Question 16 Why is 1918 an important date in the history of women's rights?

- ☐ **A** The first divorce laws were introduced.
- ☐ **B** Women over the age of 30 were given voting rights.
- ☐ **C** Equal pay laws were passed.
- ☐ **D** Women were made legally responsible for their children.

Question 17 Is the statement below ☐ TRUE or ☐ FALSE?

In 1921 a peace treaty was signed which led to Ireland becoming two countries.

Question 18 Is the statement below ☐ TRUE or ☐ FALSE?

John Constable (1776–1837) founded the modern police force in England.

Question 19 Who appoints life peers in the House of Lords?

☐ **A** The monarch

☐ **B** The Archbishop of Canterbury

☐ **C** The Speaker of the House of Commons

☐ **D** The Chief Whip

Question 20 Dunkirk is associated with which TWO events?

☐ **A** The fall of Singapore and small boats coming to the rescue

☐ **B** The D-Day landings and the fall of Singapore

☐ **C** The rescue of 300,000 men and small boats coming to the rescue

☐ **D** The fall of Singapore and the rescue of 300,000 men

Question 21 Which of the following statements is correct?

☐ **A** The Black Death caused the death of one third of people in Ireland.

☐ **B** The Black Death caused the death of one third of people in England, Scotland and Wales.

Question 22 What happens when a Member of Parliament (MP) dies or resigns?

☐ **A** The post remains vacant until the next General Election.

☐ **B** Their party chooses someone to fill the post until the next General Election.

☐ **C** A by-election is held to replace the MP.

☐ **D** A neighbouring MP looks after the constituency.

Question 23 Which festival is celebrated on 31 October?

- ☐ **A** Valentine's Day
- ☐ **B** Bonfire Night
- ☐ **C** Halloween
- ☐ **D** Hogmanay

Question 24 Is the statement below ☐ TRUE or ☐ FALSE?

Most people live in the countryside in the UK.

Answers to Practice Test 6

Question number	Answer	Explanation	Handbook chapter	Handbook page reference
1	B	Most citizens of the UK, Ireland or the Commonwealth aged 18 or over can stand for public office.	The UK government, the law and your role	Page 135
2	D	In England, Wales and Northern Ireland, serious offences are tried in front of a judge and jury in a Crown Court. In Scotland, serious cases are heard in a Sheriff Court with either a sheriff or a sheriff with a jury.	The UK government, the law and your role	Page 145
3	C	It is a criminal offence to sell alcohol to anyone who is under 18 or to buy alcohol for people who are under the age of 18. (There is one exception: people aged 16 or over can drink alcohol with a meal in a hotel or restaurant).	A modern, thriving society	Page 141
4	D	In the 19th century, the medieval 'gothic' style became popular again. The Houses of Parliament and St Pancras Station were built at this time.	A modern, thriving society	Page 96
5	C	In Scotland a jury has 15 members. In England, Wales and Northern Ireland a jury has 12 members.	The UK government, the law and your role	Page 146
6	TRUE	In 1588, the English defeated the Spanish Armada (a large fleet of ships), which had been sent by Spain to conquer England and restore Catholicism.	A long and illustrious history	Page 29

Question number	Answer	Explanation	Handbook chapter	Handbook page reference
7	D	In the UK, Mothering Sunday is celebrated on the Sunday three weeks before Easter and Father's Day on the third Sunday in June. Children send cards and give gifts on these days.	A modern, thriving society	Page 82
8	B	In the UK, people often enjoy a gamble on sports or other events. You have to be over 18 to go into betting shops or gambling clubs.	A modern, thriving society	Page 106
9	A	In 1776, 13 American colonies declared their independence from Britain, stating that people had a right to establish their own governments.	A long and illustrious history	Page 44
10	C	In the UK you need to be at least 16 years old to ride a moped.	The UK government, the law and your role	Page 152
11	B	In the 19th century, Gilbert and Sullivan wrote comic operas, often making fun of popular culture and politics. These operas include *HMS Pinafore*, *The Pirates of Penzance* and *The Mikado*.	A modern, thriving society	Page 93
12	TRUE	British society is founded on fundamental values and principles, which are based on history and traditions and are protected by law, customs and expectations.	The values and principles of the UK	Page 7
13	TRUE	In 1833 the Emancipation Act abolished slavery throughout the British Empire.	A long and illustrious history	Page 43

Question number	Answer	Explanation	Handbook chapter	Handbook page reference
14	A	Jane Austen was an English novelist. Her books include *Pride and Prejudice* and *Sense and Sensibility*. Her novels are concerned with marriage and family relationships. Many have been made into television programmes or films.	A modern, thriving society	Page 98
15	C	It is important to recycle as much of your waste as you can, so the amount of rubbish being put into landfill is reduced. Walking and using public transport to get around when you can is also a good way to protect the environment.	The UK government, the law and your role	Page 160
16	B	In 1918, women over the age of 30 were given voting rights. In 1928, women were given the right to vote at the age of 21, the same as men.	A long and illustrious history	Page 51
17	TRUE	In 1921 a peace treaty was signed and in 1922 Ireland became two countries. The six counties in the north which were mainly Protestant remained part of the UK under the name Northern Ireland. The rest of Ireland became the Irish Free State. It had its own government and became a republic in 1949.	A long and illustrious history	Page 55
18	FALSE	John Constable was a landscape painter most famous for his works of Dedham Vale on the Suffolk–Essex border in the east of England.	A modern, thriving society	Page 94
19	A	Life peers are appointed by the monarch on the advice of the Prime Minister.	The UK government, the law and your role	Page 124

Question number	Answer	Explanation	Handbook chapter	Handbook page reference
20	C	In 1940, many civilian volunteers in small pleasure and fishing boats from Britain helped the Navy to rescue 300,000 men from the beaches around Dunkirk. The evacuation gave rise to the phrase 'the Dunkirk spirit'.	A long and illustrious history	Page 58
21	B	In 1348, a disease, probably a form of plague, came to Britain. This was known as the Black Death. One third of the population of England died and a similar proportion in Scotland and Wales.	A long and illustrious history	Page 22
22	C	If an MP dies or resigns, there will be a fresh election, called a by-election, in his or her constituency.	The UK government, the law and your role	Page 125
23	C	Halloween is celebrated on 31 October.	A modern, thriving society	Page 82
24	FALSE	Most people in the UK live in towns and cities, but much of Britain is still countryside.	A modern, thriving society	Page 71

Practice Test 7

Question 1 Is the statement below ☐ TRUE or ☐ FALSE?

The 40 days before Easter are known as Lent.

Question 2 Which of the following statements is correct?

☐ **A** Magistrates usually work unpaid and do not need legal qualifications.

☐ **B** Magistrates must be specially trained legal experts who have been solicitors for three years.

Question 3 Which TWO were 20th-century British discoveries or inventions?

☐ **A** Mobile phones and walkmans

☐ **B** Cashpoints (ATMs) and walkmans

☐ **C** Cloning a mammal and cashpoints (ATMs)

☐ **D** Cloning a mammal and mobile phones

Question 4 Who do some local councils appoint as a ceremonial leader?

☐ **A** A local business leader

☐ **B** A member of the Royal Family

☐ **C** A local celebrity

☐ **D** A mayor

Question 5 With which sport do you associate Lewis Hamilton, Jenson Button and Damon Hill?

☐ **A** Football

☐ **B** Athletics

☐ **C** Skiing

☐ **D** Formula 1

Question 6   Is the statement below ☐ TRUE or ☐ FALSE?

A public vote in 2002 decided that Winston Churchill was the greatest Briton of all time.

Question 7   What happens when Members of Parliament (MPs) hold surgeries?

☐ **A** Local councillors meet their MP to discuss local issues.

☐ **B** Members of the public meet their MP to discuss issues.

☐ **C** MPs meet doctors to discuss local health issues.

☐ **D** MPs meet the press to discuss national issues.

Question 8   Which of the following UK landmarks is in Northern Ireland?

☐ **A** Big Ben

☐ **B** Snowdonia

☐ **C** The Giant's Causeway

☐ **D** The Eden Project

Question 9   What task is associated with the National Trust?

☐ **A** Building new public roads

☐ **B** Preserving old aircraft

☐ **C** Preserving important buildings and places

☐ **D** Managing investment accounts

Question 10 Which of the following is a fundamental principle of British life?

☐ **A** Extremism

☐ **B** Individual liberty

☐ **C** Intolerance

☐ **D** Inequality

Question 11 Which of the following statements is correct?

☐ **A** In Elizabeth I's time, English settlers began to colonise Australia.

☐ **B** In Elizabeth I's time, English settlers began to colonise the eastern coast of America.

Question 12 Which of the following statements is correct?

☐ **A** Members of the House of Lords are not elected by the people.

☐ **B** Members of the House of Lords are voted in by members of the House of Commons.

Question 13 In which battle during the First World War did the British suffer 60,000 casualties on the first day?

☐ **A** Agincourt

☐ **B** El Alamein

☐ **C** The Somme

☐ **D** Waterloo

Question 14 Is the statement below ☐ TRUE OR ☐ FALSE?

Members of the public are allowed to attend Youth Court hearings.

Question 15 Which of the following statements is correct?

☐ **A** A famous sailing event is held at Cowes on the Isle of Wight.

☐ **B** A famous sailing event is held in the city of Norwich.

Question 16 During which part of the year are pantomime productions staged in theatres?

☐ **A** Easter

☐ **B** Summer

☐ **C** Christmas

☐ **D** Valentine's Day

Question 17 Is the statement below ☐ TRUE or ☐ FALSE?

'The Restoration' refers to the re-establishment of Catholicism as the official Church in the 17th century.

Question 18 Is the statement below ☐ TRUE or ☐ FALSE?

Members of the armed forces cannot stand for public office.

Question 19 Which TWO political parties formed the coalition government in 2010?

☐ **A** Labour and Chartists

☐ **B** Chartists and Liberal Democrats

☐ **C** Conservatives and Liberal Democrats

☐ **D** Conservatives and Labour

Question 20 How often are Members of Parliament (MPs) elected?

- [ ] **A** At least every three years
- [ ] **B** Every six months
- [ ] **C** Every year
- [ ] **D** At least every five years

Question 21 In the 19th century, the UK produced more than half the world's supply of one of these products. Which one?

- [ ] **A** Cotton cloth
- [ ] **B** Beer
- [ ] **C** Cigarettes
- [ ] **D** Rubber

Question 22 Is the statement below ☐ TRUE or ☐ FALSE?

Most people in the UK live in towns and cities.

Question 23 Which TWO courts deal with minor criminal cases in the UK?

- [ ] **A** Justice of the Peace Court and Magistrates' Court
- [ ] **B** Centre Court and Crown Court
- [ ] **C** Justice of the Peace Court and Crown Court
- [ ] **D** Crown Court and Magistrates' Court

Question 24 Once you are aged 17, which TWO vehicles can you learn to drive?

- [ ] **A** Car and fire engine
- [ ] **B** Motor cycle and fire engine
- [ ] **C** Motor cycle and heavy goods vehicle
- [ ] **D** Motor cycle and car

Answers to Practice Test 7

Question number	Answer	Explanation	Handbook chapter	Handbook page reference
1	TRUE	Lent is a time when Christians take time to reflect and prepare for Easter. Traditionally, people would fast during this period and today many people will give something up, like a favourite food.	A modern, thriving society	Page 80
2	A	Magistrates are members of the local community. They usually work unpaid and do not need legal qualifications.	The UK government, the law and your role	Pages 144–5
3	C	In 1996 Sir Ian Wilmut and Keith Campbell led a team which was the first to succeed in cloning a mammal. In the 1960s James Goodfellow invented the cashpoint (ATM).	A long and illustrious history	Page 65
4	D	Many local authorities appoint a mayor, who is the ceremonial leader of the council. (In some towns, a mayor is elected to be the effective leader of the administration.)	The UK government, the law and your role	Page 129
5	D	Lewis Hamilton, Jenson Button and Damon Hill are all British Grand Prix drivers who have won the Formula 1 World Championship.	A modern, thriving society	Page 89
6	TRUE	In 2002, Winston Churchill (1874–1965) was voted the greatest Briton of all time by the public.	A long and illustrious history	Page 57
7	B	Many MPs hold regular local 'surgeries', where constituents can go in person to talk about issues that are of concern to them.	The UK government, the law and your role	Page 126

Question number	Answer	Explanation	Handbook chapter	Handbook page reference
8	C	Located on the north-east coast of Northern Ireland, the Giant's Causeway is a land formation of columns made from volcanic lava.	A modern, thriving society	Page 184
9	C	Many parts of the countryside and places of interest are kept open by the National Trust in England, Wales and Northern Ireland and the National Trust for Scotland. Both are charities that work to preserve important buildings, coastline and countryside in the UK.	A modern, thriving society	Page 107
10	B	Individual liberty is a fundamental principle of British life. There is no place in British society for extremism or intolerance.	The values and principles of the UK	Page 7
11	B	In Elizabeth I's time, English settlers first began to colonise the eastern coast of America.	A long and illustrious history	Page 30
12	A	Members of the House of Lords are not elected by the people and do not represent a constituency.	The UK government, the law and your role	Page 124
13	C	In July 1916 the British suffered 60,000 casualties on the first day of the Battle of the Somme.	A long and illustrious history	Page 54
14	FALSE	Members of the public are not allowed in Youth Courts, and the name or photographs of the accused young person cannot be published in newspapers or used by the media.	The UK government, the law and your role	Page 146
15	A	Many sailing events are held throughout the UK, the most famous of which is at Cowes on the Isle of Wight.	A modern, thriving society	Page 89

Question number	Answer	Explanation	Handbook chapter	Handbook page reference
16	C	Many theatres produce a pantomime at Christmas time. They are light-hearted plays with music and comedy, enjoyed by family audiences.	A modern, thriving society	Page 93
17	FALSE	In May 1660, Parliament invited Charles II to come back from exile in the Netherlands. He was crowned King Charles II of England, Wales, Scotland and Ireland. This is referred to as 'The Restoration'.	A long and illustrious history	Page 34
18	TRUE	Most citizens of the UK, Ireland or the Commonwealth aged 18 or over can stand for public office. There are some exceptions, including members of the armed forces.	The UK government, the law and your role	Page 135
19	C	In May 2010, the Conservative and Liberal Democrat parties formed a coalition and the leader of the Conservative Party, David Cameron, became Prime Minister.	A long and illustrious history	Page 69
20	D	MPs are elected at a General Election, which is held at least every five years.	The UK government, the law and your role	Page 125
21	A	In the 19th century the UK produced more than half of the world's supplies of iron, coal and cotton cloth.	A long and illustrious history	Page 48
22	TRUE	Most people live in towns and cities but much of Britain is still countryside.	A modern, thriving society	Page 71
23	A	In England, Wales and Northern Ireland, most minor criminal cases are dealt with in a Magistrates' Court. In Scotland, minor criminal offences go to a Justice of the Peace Court.	The UK government, the law and your role	Page 144

Question number	Answer	Explanation	Handbook chapter	Handbook page reference
24	D	In the UK, you must be at least 17 years old to drive a car or motor cycle and you must have a driving licence to drive on public roads.	The UK government, the law and your role	Page 152

Practice Test 8

Question 1   Which of the following statements is correct?

☐ **A** Most shops in the UK open seven days a week.

☐ **B** All shops in the UK close on Sundays.

Question 2   Which of these is a fundamental principle of British life?

☐ **A** Actively supporting your local football team

☐ **B** Participation in community life

☐ **C** Ignoring your neighbours

☐ **D** Eating fish on a Friday

Question 3   Who were the 'suffragettes'?

☐ **A** Women who left the UK to live in America

☐ **B** Women who campaigned for women's votes

☐ **C** Women who left their jobs when they got married

☐ **D** Women who stayed at home to raise a family

Question 4   Which of the following statements is correct?

☐ **A** Members of Parliament (MPs) are elected through a system called 'first past the post'.

☐ **B** MPs are elected through a system called 'proportional representation'.

Question 5 Which TWO of the following are responsibilities of Members of Parliament (MPs)?

☐ **A** Representing everyone in their constituency and supporting the government on all decisions and laws

☐ **B** Scrutinising and commenting on what the government is doing and representing only those who voted for them

☐ **C** Scrutinising and commenting on what the government is doing and supporting the government on all decisions and laws

☐ **D** Representing everyone in their constituency and scrutinising and commenting on what the government is doing

Question 6 Which of the following statements is correct?

☐ **A** National parks are areas of protected countryside that everyone can visit.

☐ **B** National parks are national sports stadiums for people to hold sporting events.

Question 7 Is the statement below ☐ TRUE or ☐ FALSE?

Northern Ireland and Scotland have their own banknotes.

Question 8 Which of the following statements is correct?

☐ **A** In Northern Ireland a member of your family must complete a voting registration form on your behalf.

☐ **B** In Northern Ireland all those entitled to vote must complete their own registration form.

Question 9   Is the statement below ☐ TRUE or ☐ FALSE?

On average, boys in the UK leave school with better qualifications than girls.

Question 10   Which of the following was Isambard Kingdom Brunel famous for building?

☐ **A** Motor cars
☐ **B** Aeroplanes
☐ **C** Bridges
☐ **D** Skyscrapers

Question 11   Which TWO of the following do you have to pay tax on?

☐ **A** Income from property, savings and dividends, and small amounts of money given to you as a gift
☐ **B** Income from property, savings and dividends, and shopping vouchers given to you by family or friends
☐ **C** Profits from self-employment, and income from property, savings and dividends
☐ **D** Profits from self-employment, and shopping vouchers given to you by family or friends

Question 12   Is the statement below ☐ TRUE or ☐ FALSE?

Pantomimes are plays based on fairy stories.

Question 13   What must police officers do?

☐ **A** Be rude and abusive
☐ **B** Obey the law
☐ **C** Make a false statement
☐ **D** Commit racial discrimination

Question 14 Why was the Magna Carta important?

☐ **A** It gave all men the vote.

☐ **B** It restricted the power of the monarch.

☐ **C** It established a system of free education.

☐ **D** It gave women legal rights.

Question 15 By joining a political party, what TWO activities might you be involved in?

☐ **A** Violent clashes with other political parties, and handing out leaflets in the street

☐ **B** Joining your MPs for sessions in the House of Commons, and handing out leaflets in the street

☐ **C** Handing out leaflets in the street, and knocking on people's doors asking for support

☐ **D** Joining your MP for sessions in the House of Commons, and knocking on people's doors and asking for support

Question 16 Is the statement below ☐ TRUE or ☐ FALSE?

In the UK, there are now a record number of people aged 85 and over.

Question 17 Which TWO of these figures were great Scottish thinkers of the Enlightenment?

☐ **A** Robert Louis Stevenson and David Hume

☐ **B** Adam Smith and David Hume

☐ **C** Robert Burns and Robert Louis Stevenson

☐ **D** Robert Burns and David Hume

Question 18 Is the statement below ☐ TRUE or ☐ FALSE?

Margaret Thatcher was the longest-serving UK
Prime Minister of the 20th century.

Question 19 During which period did agriculture and the manufacturing of goods become mechanised?

☐ **A** The Glorious Revolution

☐ **B** The Industrial Revolution

☐ **C** The Middle Ages

☐ **D** The Bronze Age

Question 20 In 1999, what happened to hereditary peers in the House of Lords?

☐ **A** Their numbers were greatly increased.

☐ **B** Their salaries were stopped.

☐ **C** Women were allowed to inherit their titles.

☐ **D** They lost their automatic right to attend the House of Lords.

Question 21 Is the statement below ☐ TRUE or ☐ FALSE?

Pressure and lobby groups try to influence government policy.

Question 22 What is one of the roles of school governors?

☐ **A** Setting the strategic direction of the school

☐ **B** Marking students' homework

☐ **C** Giving teachers ideas for lesson plans

☐ **D** Serving food and drink in the canteen

Question 23 Which of the following statements is correct?

☐ **A** Several British writers have won the Nobel Prize in Literature.

☐ **B** No British writer has won the Nobel Prize in Literature.

Question 24 Which parts of the United Kingdom have devolved governments?

☐ **A** England and Wales

☐ **B** Wales, England and Northern Ireland

☐ **C** Only Northern Ireland

☐ **D** Wales, Scotland and Northern Ireland

Answers to Practice Test 8

Question number	Answer	Explanation	Handbook chapter	Handbook page reference
1	A	Most shops in the UK open seven days a week, although trading hours on Sundays and public holidays are generally reduced.	A modern, thriving society	Page 102
2	B	Participation in community life is one of the fundamental values and principles which all those living in the UK should respect and support.	The values and principles of the UK	Page 8
3	B	In the late 19th and early 20th centuries, an increasing number of women campaigned and demonstrated for women's rights, in particular the right to vote. They formed the women's suffrage movement and became known as 'suffragettes'.	A long and illustrious history	Page 51
4	A	MPs are elected through a system called 'first past the post'. This means that in each constituency, the candidate who gets the most votes is elected.	The UK government, the law and your role	Page 125
5	D	MPs have a number of different responsibilities, including representing everyone in their constituency, and scrutinising and commenting on what the government is doing.	The UK government, the law and your role	Page 124
6	A	National parks are areas of protected countryside that everyone can visit, and where people live, work and look after the landscape. There are 15 national parks in England, Wales and Scotland.	A modern, thriving society	Page 107

Question number	Answer	Explanation	Handbook chapter	Handbook page reference
7	TRUE	Northern Ireland and Scotland have their own banknotes, which are valid everywhere in the UK.	A modern, thriving society	Page 74
8	B	Northern Ireland has a system called 'individual registration', which means all those entitled to vote must complete their own registration form.	The UK government, the law and your role	Page 134
9	FALSE	On average, girls leave school with better qualifications than boys. Also, more women than men study at university.	A modern, thriving society	Page 75
10	C	Isambard Kingdom Brunel was a famous Victorian engineer who built railway lines, bridges, tunnels and ships.	A long and illustrious history	Page 48
11	C	People in the UK have to pay tax on their income, which includes profits from self-employment, and income from property, savings and dividends. Money raised from income tax pays for government services such as roads, education, police and the armed forces.	The UK government, the law and your role	Page 151
12	TRUE	Pantomime plays are a British tradition. Many theatres produce a pantomime at Christmas time. They are based on fairy stories and are light-hearted plays with music and comedy.	A modern, thriving society	Page 93
13	B	Police officers must obey the law. They must not be rude or abusive, make a false statement, misuse their authority, or commit racial discrimination.	The UK government, the law and your role	Page 142

Question number	Answer	Explanation	Handbook chapter	Handbook page reference
14	B	King John was forced by his noblemen to agree to a number of demands. The result was a charter of rights called the Magna Carta, which restricted the king's power to collect taxes or to make or change laws.	A long and illustrious history	Page 22
15	C	Political parties welcome new members. Members work hard to persuade people to vote for their candidates – for instance, by handing out leaflets in the street or by knocking on people's doors and asking for their support. This is called 'canvassing'.	The UK government, the law and your role	Pages 156–7
16	TRUE	People in the UK are living longer than ever before. There are now a record number of people aged 85 and over.	A modern, thriving society	Page 75
17	B	Many of the great thinkers of the Enlightenment were Scottish. Adam Smith developed ideas about economics. David Hume wrote about human nature.	A long and illustrious history	Page 40
18	TRUE	Margaret Thatcher was the longest-serving Prime Minister of the 20th century. She won her first General Election in 1979 and was re-elected in 1983 and 1987. She left office in 1990.	A long and illustrious history	Page 67
19	B	The Industrial Revolution was the rapid development of industry in Britain in the 18th and 19th centuries. Britain was the first country to industrialise on a large scale. It happened because of the development of machinery and the use of steam power. Agriculture and the manufacturing of goods became mechanised.	A long and illustrious history	Pages 40–2

Question number	Answer	Explanation	Handbook chapter	Handbook page reference
20	D	Since 1999, hereditary peers have lost the automatic right to attend the House of Lords. They now elect a few of their number to represent them in the House of Lords.	The UK government, the law and your role	Page 124
21	TRUE	Pressure and lobby groups are organisations which try to influence government policy. They play an important role in politics.	The UK government, the law and your role	Page 128
22	A	School governors have an important part to play in raising school standards. This includes setting the strategic direction of the school.	The UK government, the law and your role	Page 156
23	A	Several British writers, including the novelist Sir William Golding, the poet Seamus Heaney, and the playwright Harold Pinter, have won the Nobel Prize in Literature.	A modern, thriving society	Page 97
24	D	Some powers have been devolved from central government to give people in Wales, Scotland and Northern Ireland more control over matters that directly affect them.	The UK government, the law and your role	Page 129

Practice Test 9

Question 1 Which of the following statements is correct?

☐ **A** Mary, Queen of Scots was a Catholic.

☐ **B** Mary, Queen of Scots was a Protestant.

Question 2 How often does Prime Minister's Questions occur when Parliament is sitting?

☐ **A** Every day

☐ **B** Twice a week

☐ **C** Once a week

☐ **D** Once a month

Question 3 Which TWO of the following are recent British film actors that have won Oscars?

☐ **A** Tilda Swinton and Jayne Torvill

☐ **B** Colin Firth and Robert Louis Stevenson

☐ **C** Jayne Torvill and Colin Firth

☐ **D** Tilda Swinton and Colin Firth

Question 4 Who was given the title of Lord Protector in the 17th century?

☐ **A** King Charles II

☐ **B** Samuel Pepys

☐ **C** Oliver Cromwell

☐ **D** Isaac Newton

Question 5 The term 'D-Day' refers to which event in British history?

☐ **A** The Battle of Trafalgar

☐ **B** Landing of allied troops in Normandy

☐ **C** Dropping of the atom bomb on Japan

☐ **D** End of the war in Europe in 1945

Question 6 Which of the following statements is correct?

☐ **A** Proceedings in Parliament cannot be reported in the press.

☐ **B** Proceedings in Parliament are broadcast on television.

Question 7 Which TWO foods are associated with England?

☐ **A** Ulster fry and roast beef

☐ **B** Haggis and roast beef

☐ **C** Roast beef, and fish and chips

☐ **D** Haggis and Ulster fry

Question 8 Which jubilee did Queen Elizabeth II celebrate in 2012?

☐ **A** Platinum Jubilee (70 years as Queen)

☐ **B** Diamond Jubilee (60 years as Queen)

☐ **C** Silver Jubilee (25 years as Queen)

☐ **D** Golden Jubilee (50 years as Queen)

Question 9   Which of the following statements is correct?

  ☐ **A** Rugby was introduced to ancient Britain by Viking invaders.

  ☐ **B** Rugby originated in England in the early 19th century.

Question 10   Which queen is remembered for fighting against the Romans?

  ☐ **A** Elizabeth

  ☐ **B** Boudicca

  ☐ **C** Victoria

  ☐ **D** Anne

Question 11   Which TWO of the following are Christian groups?

  ☐ **A** Roman Catholics and Baptists

  ☐ **B** Hindus and Baptists

  ☐ **C** Roman Catholics and Sikhs

  ☐ **D** Roman Catholics and Buddhists

Question 12   Is the statement below ☐ TRUE or ☐ FALSE?

  When Queen Anne died in 1714, parliament chose a German to be the next king of England.

Question 13   Which of the following statements is correct?

  ☐ **A** There is a yearly sailing race on the River Thames between Oxford and Cambridge Universities.

  ☐ **B** There is a yearly rowing race on the River Thames between Oxford and Cambridge Universities.

Question 14 Is the statement below ☐ TRUE or ☐ FALSE?

You can support your local community by becoming a school governor.

Question 15 Which of the following statements is correct?

☐ **A** Richard Arkwright developed new farming methods in the UK.

☐ **B** Richard Arkwright ran efficient and profitable factories.

Question 16 What do Sir William Golding, Seamus Heaney and Harold Pinter have in common?

☐ **A** They were all famous British athletes.

☐ **B** They all became Prime Minister.

☐ **C** They were part of the first British expedition to the North Pole.

☐ **D** They have all won the Nobel Prize in Literature.

Question 17 Which of the following statements is correct?

☐ **A** The UK offers its citizens and permanent residents freedom of speech.

☐ **B** The UK does not allow citizens or permanent residents to voice opinions publicly.

Question 18 Which part of the UK is associated with Robert Burns (1759–96)?

☐ **A** England

☐ **B** Scotland

☐ **C** Wales

☐ **D** Northern Ireland

Question 19 Is the statement below ☐ TRUE or ☐ FALSE?

*Hereditary peers have the automatic right
to attend the House of Lords.*

Question 20 Which of the following statements is correct?

☐ **A** Sake Dean Mahomet is famous for introducing tea-drinking and bungalows to Britain from India.

☐ **B** Sake Dean Mahomet is famous for introducing curry houses to Britain from India.

Question 21 The term 'suffragettes' is associated with which group of people?

☐ **A** Men

☐ **B** Women

☐ **C** Children

☐ **D** Migrants

Question 22 Which TWO of the following were famous Victorians?

☐ **A** Isambard Kingdom Brunel and Margaret Thatcher

☐ **B** Isambard Kingdom Brunel and Florence Nightingale

☐ **C** Margaret Thatcher and Dylan Thomas

☐ **D** Margaret Thatcher and Florence Nightingale

Question 23 Which TWO of the following do pressure and lobby groups do?

☐ **A** Organise violent protests and try to influence government policy

☐ **B** Assist MPs in their constituency work and represent the views of British business

☐ **C** Try to influence government policy and represent the views of British businesses

☐ **D** Organise violent protests and assist MPs in their constituency work

Question 24 What is a fundamental principle of British life?

☐ **A** The rule of law

☐ **B** The rule of the upper classes

☐ **C** The rule of the monarch

☐ **D** The rule of your local Member of Parliament (MP)

Answers to Practice Test 9

Question number	Answer	Explanation	Handbook chapter	Handbook page reference
1	B	The queen of Scotland, Mary Stuart (often now called 'Mary, Queen of Scots') was a Catholic.	A long and illustrious history	Page 29
2	C	Prime Minister's Questions takes place every week while Parliament is sitting.	The UK government, the law and your role	Page 128
3	D	Recent British actors to have won Oscars include Colin Firth, Sir Antony Hopkins, Dame Judi Dench, Kate Winslet and Tilda Swinton.	A modern, thriving society	Page 104
4	C	Oliver Cromwell was given the title of Lord Protector and ruled until his death in 1658.	A long and illustrious history	Page 34
5	B	On 6 June 1944 (often referred to as 'D-Day'), allied forces landed in Normandy. Following victory on the beaches of Normandy, the allied forces pressed on through France and eventually into Germany.	A long and illustrious history	Page 59
6	B	Proceedings in Parliament are broadcast on television and published in official reports called Hansard. Most people get information about political issues and events from newspapers (often called 'the press'), television, radio and the internet.	The UK government, the law and your role	Page 132
7	C	Roast beef is served with potatoes, vegetables, Yorkshire puddings and other accompaniments. Fish and chips are also popular in England.	A modern, thriving society	Page 102

Question number	Answer	Explanation	Handbook chapter	Handbook page reference
8	B	Queen Elizabeth II has reigned since her father's death in 1952, and in 2012 she celebrated her Diamond Jubilee (60 years as queen).	The UK government, the law and your role	Page 121
9	B	Rugby originated in England in the early 19th century and is a very popular sport in the UK today.	A modern, thriving society	Page 88
10	B	One of the tribal leaders who fought against the Romans was Boudicca, the queen of the Iceni in what is now eastern England. She is still remembered today and there is a statue of her on Westminster Bridge in London, near the Houses of Parliament.	A long and illustrious history	Page 17
11	A	Roman Catholics and Baptists are Christian groups. Baptists are a Protestant Christian group. Other Protestant groups include the Church of England, Methodists, Presbyterians and Quakers.	A modern, thriving society	Page 184
12	TRUE	Queen Anne had no surviving children, so Parliament chose a German, George I, to be the next king, because he was Anne's nearest Protestant relative.	A long and illustrious history	Page 39
13	B	Rowing is a popular sport in the UK, both as a leisure activity and as a competitive sport. There is a popular yearly race on the River Thames between Oxford and Cambridge Universities.	A modern, thriving society	Page 89
14	TRUE	School governors are people from the local community who wish to make a positive contribution to children's education.	The UK government, the law and your role	Page 156

Question number	Answer	Explanation	Handbook chapter	Handbook page reference
15	B	Richard Arkwright is remembered for the efficient and profitable way that he ran his factories.	A long and illustrious history	Page 41
16	D	Several British writers, including the novelist Sir William Golding, the poet Seamus Heaney, and the playwright Harold Pinter, have won the Nobel Prize in Literature.	A modern, thriving society	Page 97
17	A	The UK offers citizens and permanent residents various freedoms and rights, including freedom of speech.	The values and principles of the UK	Page 8
18	B	Robert Burns is associated with Scotland. He was a poet. One of his best-known works is the song *Auld Lang Syne*.	A long and illustrious history	Page 40
19	FALSE	Since 1999, hereditary peers have lost the automatic right to attend the House of Lords. They now elect a few of their number to represent them.	The UK government, the law and your role	Page 124
20	B	Sake Dean Mahomet (1759–1851) opened the first curry house in Britain in 1810.	A long and illustrious history	Page 42
21	B	In the late 19th and early 20th centuries, an increasing number of women campaigned and demonstrated for greater rights and, in particular, the right to vote. They formed the women's suffrage movement and became known as 'suffragettes'.	A long and illustrious history	Page 50
22	B	Isambard Kingdom Brunel (1806–59) was a famous engineer, and Florence Nightingale (1820–1910) established a training school for nurses, the first of its kind.	A long and illustrious history	Page 48

Question number	Answer	Explanation	Handbook chapter	Handbook page reference
23	C	Pressure and lobby groups are organisations which try to influence government policy. Some represent the views of British business. Others campaign on particular topics, such as the environment.	The UK government, the law and your role	Page 128
24	A	The rule of law is a fundamental principle of British life. British society is founded on fundamental values and principles which all those living in the UK should respect and support.	The values and principles of the UK	Page 7

Practice Test 10

Question 1 Is the statement below ☐ TRUE or ☐ FALSE?

Shakespeare was a playwright and actor.

Question 2 Which TWO of the following are famous British film directors?

☐ **A** Sir Alfred Hitchcock and Evelyn Waugh

☐ **B** Evelyn Waugh and Thomas Gainsborough

☐ **C** Sir Alfred Hitchcock and Sir Ridley Scott

☐ **D** Evelyn Waugh and Sir Ridley Scott

Question 3 Is the statement below ☐ TRUE or ☐ FALSE?

Sir Isaac Newton was a famous musician from the 18th century.

Question 4 Which TWO of the following would you contact for help on a legal matter?

☐ **A** A solicitor and Citizens Advice

☐ **B** A solicitor and a local councillor

☐ **C** A local councillor and your local Member of Parliament (MP)

☐ **D** Citizens Advice and your local Member of Parliament (MP)

Question 5 Which TWO new national bodies began operating in 1999?

☐ **A** Welsh Assembly (now called the Senedd and Scottish Parliament

☐ **B** Scottish Parliament and English Parliament

☐ **C** House of Lords and Welsh Assembly (now called the Senedd)

☐ **D** House of Lords and Scottish Parliament

Question 6 Which of the following statements is correct?

☐ **A** Sir Andy Murray is the first British man to sail around the world.

☐ **B** Sir Andy Murray is the first British man to win a singles tennis title in a Grand Slam tournament since 1936.

Question 7 Which TWO are associated with Sir Francis Drake?

☐ **A** Defeating the Spanish Armada and early flight

☐ **B** Defeating the Spanish Armada and sailing around the world

☐ **C** Early flight and the Titanic

☐ **D** The Titanic and sailing around the world

Question 8 Which of the following is a responsibility you will have as a citizen or permanent resident of the UK?

☐ **A** Using your car as much as possible

☐ **B** Visiting your local pub regularly

☐ **C** Keeping an allotment

☐ **D** Looking after the area in which you live and the environment

Question 9 Which TWO of the following are famous British authors?

☐ **A** Gustav Holst and J K Rowling

☐ **B** Sir Steve Redgrave and Sir Arthur Conan Doyle

☐ **C** Sir Steve Redgrave and Gustav Holst

☐ **D** Sir Arthur Conan Doyle and J K Rowling

Question 10 Is the statement below ☐ TRUE OR ☐ FALSE?

The British constitution is contained in a single written document.

Question 11 Which TWO people are famous UK sports stars?

☐ **A** Sir Chris Hoy and Dame Kelly Holmes

☐ **B** Lucien Freud and Jane Austen

☐ **C** Dame Kelly Holmes and Jane Austen

☐ **D** Sir Chris Hoy and Lucien Freud

Question 12 Which of the following statements is correct?

☐ **A** The first person to use the title Prime Minister was Sir Robert Walpole.

☐ **B** The first person to use the title Prime Minister was Sir Christopher Wren.

Question 13 Why is Sir Edwin Lutyens famous?

☐ **A** He won a gold medal at the London 2012 Olympic Games.

☐ **B** He was the first UK Prime Minister.

☐ **C** He invented the World Wide Web.

☐ **D** He was a 20th-century architect.

Question 14 Is the statement below ☐ TRUE or ☐ FALSE?

Sir Mo Farah and Dame Jessica Ennis-Hill are well-known athletes who won gold medals at the 2012 London Olympics.

Question 15 What did St Augustine and St Columba do during the Anglo-Saxon period?

- [ ] **A** They invented new farming techniques.
- [ ] **B** They led an uprising in Wales.
- [ ] **C** They helped to spread Christianity across Britain.
- [ ] **D** They fought courageously against the Romans.

Question 16 Which of the following statements is correct?

- [ ] **A** The Chancellor of the Exchequer is responsible for crime, policing and immigration.
- [ ] **B** The Chancellor of the Exchequer is responsible for the economy.

Question 17 Is the statement below ☐ TRUE or ☐ FALSE?

In the 1830s and 1840s a group called the Chartists campaigned for reform to the voting system.

Question 18 Which of the following is a Stone Age monument in the UK?

- [ ] **A** Globe Theatre
- [ ] **B** Nelson's Column
- [ ] **C** Stonehenge
- [ ] **D** Windsor Castle

Question 19 Is the statement below ☐ TRUE or ☐ FALSE?

Snowdonia is a national park in Northern Ireland.

Question 20 Which TWO are famous gardens in the UK?

☐ **A** Sissinghurst and Snowdonia

☐ **B** London Eye and Sissinghurst

☐ **C** London Eye and Snowdonia

☐ **D** Sissinghurst and Bodnant Garden

Question 21 Which of the following statements is correct?

☐ **A** The 'Swinging Sixties' was a period of religious change.

☐ **B** The 'Swinging Sixties' was a period of social change.

Question 22 Which TWO groups were associated with King Charles I and Parliament during the English Civil War?

☐ **A** Tories and Roundheads

☐ **B** Cavaliers and Luddites

☐ **C** Roundheads and Cavaliers

☐ **D** Roundheads and Luddites

Question 23 St Andrew is the patron saint of which country?

☐ **A** England

☐ **B** Scotland

☐ **C** Wales

☐ **D** Northern Ireland

Question 24 Which of the following statements is correct?

☐ **A** Plymouth, Norwich and Leeds are cities in England.

☐ **B** Newport, Swansea and Cardiff are cities in Scotland.

Answers to Practice Test 10

Question number	Answer	Explanation	Handbook chapter	Handbook page reference
1	TRUE	Shakespeare was born in Stratford-upon-Avon, England. He was a playwright and actor and wrote many poems and plays.	A long and illustrious history	Page 30
2	C	Sir Alfred Hitchcock and Sir Ridley Scott are British film directors who have had great success in the UK and internationally.	A modern, thriving society	Page 103
3	FALSE	Sir Isaac Newton was a famous scientist who showed how gravity applied to the whole universe.	A long and illustrious history	Page 35
4	A	Solicitors are trained lawyers who give advice on legal matters, take action for their clients and represent their clients in court. Citizens Advice can give you names of local solicitors and tell you which areas of law they specialise in.	The UK government, the law and your role	Page 147
5	A	Since 1997, some powers have been devolved from the central government to give people in Wales, Scotland and Northern Ireland more control over matters that directly affect them. There has been a Welsh Assembly (now called the Senedd) and a Scottish Parliament since 1999.	A long and illustrious history	Page 129
6	B	Sir Andy Murray is a Scottish tennis player and the first British man to win a singles tennis title in a Grand Slam tournament since 1936.	A modern, thriving society	Page 86

Question number	Answer	Explanation	Handbook chapter	Handbook page reference
7	B	Sir Francis Drake was one of the commanders in the defeat of the Spanish Armada. His ship, the *Golden Hind*, was one of the first to sail right around ('circumnavigate') the world.	A long and illustrious history	Page 29
8	D	There are responsibilities and freedoms which are shared by all those living in the UK. These include looking after the area in which you live and the environment.	The values and principles of the UK	Page 8
9	D	Sir Arthur Conan Doyle was a Scottish doctor and writer. He was best known for his stories about Sherlock Holmes, who was one of the first fictional detectives. J K Rowling wrote the Harry Potter series of children's books, which have enjoyed huge international success. She now writes fiction for adults as well.	A modern, thriving society	Page 98
10	FALSE	The British constitution is not written down in any single document, and therefore it is described as 'unwritten'.	The UK government, the law and your role	Page 120
11	A	Sir Chris Hoy is a Scottish cyclist who has won six gold and one silver Olympic medals. Dame Kelly Holmes won two gold medals for running in the 2004 Olympic Games.	A modern, thriving society	Page 85
12	A	Sir Robert Walpole was the first person to be called Prime Minister. He was Prime Minister from 1721 until 1742.	A long and illustrious history	Page 39
13	D	Sir Edwin Lutyens was a famous 20th-century architect who designed the Cenotaph in Whitehall.	A modern, thriving society	Page 96

Question number	Answer	Explanation	Handbook chapter	Handbook page reference
14	TRUE	Sir Mo Farah won gold medals in the 5,000 and 10,000 metres, and Dame Jessica Ennis-Hill won a gold medal in the heptathlon.	A modern, thriving society	Page 86
15	C	St Augustine and St Columba were early Christian missionaries who came to Britain to preach about Christianity. St Columba founded a monastery on the Isle of Iona. St Augustine spread Christianity in the south and became the first Archbishop of Canterbury.	A long and illustrious history	Page 19
16	B	The Chancellor of the Exchequer is the cabinet minister responsible for the economy.	The UK government, the law and your role	Page 127
17	TRUE	The Chartists campaigned for reform of the voting system. The changes they wanted included elections every year and for all regions to be equal in the electoral system.	The UK government, the law and your role	Page 120
18	C	Stonehenge is a Stone Age monument in the English county of Wiltshire. It was probably a special gathering place for seasonal ceremonies.	A long and illustrious history	Page 15
19	FALSE	Snowdonia is a national park in North Wales. Its most well-known landmark is Snowdon, which is the highest mountain in Wales.	A modern, thriving society	Page 114
20	D	Sissinghurst is in England and Bodnant Garden is in Wales.	A modern, thriving society	Page 101

Question number	Answer	Explanation	Handbook chapter	Handbook page reference
21	B	The 1960s was a period of significant social change. It was known as 'the Swinging Sixties'. There was growth in British fashion, cinema and popular music.	A long and illustrious history	Page 63
22	C	Supporters of the king were known as Cavaliers and supporters of Parliament were known as Roundheads.	A long and illustrious history	Page 33
23	B	St Andrew is the patron saint of Scotland, and is celebrated on 30 November each year.	A modern, thriving society	Page 77
24	A	Plymouth, Norwich and Leeds are cities in England.	A modern, thriving society	Page 72

Practice Test 11

Question 1 Which of the following statements is correct?

☐ **A** Sir Steve Redgrave is a famous rower who won gold medals in five consecutive Olympic Games.

☐ **B** Sir Steve Redgrave is a famous film actor who has won several BAFTAs.

Question 2 Which TWO values are upheld by the Commonwealth association of countries?

☐ **A** Democracy and rule of law

☐ **B** Violence and rule of law

☐ **C** Democracy and communism

☐ **D** Communism and rule of law

Question 3 Which TWO are 20th-century British inventions?

☐ **A** The World Wide Web and the diesel engine

☐ **B** Television and the World Wide Web

☐ **C** Mobile phones and the diesel engine

☐ **D** Television and mobile phones

Question 4 Which of the following statements is correct?

☐ **A** The Battle of Britain in 1940 was fought at sea.

☐ **B** The Battle of Britain in 1940 was fought in the air.

Question 5 Which TWO issues can the devolved administrations pass laws on?

☐ **A** Health and foreign affairs

☐ **B** Health and education

☐ **C** Education and immigration

☐ **D** Foreign affairs and immigration

Question 6   Is the statement below ☐ TRUE or ☐ FALSE?

The Home Secretary is the government minister responsible for managing relationships with foreign countries.

Question 7   Textile and engineering firms found workers from which TWO countries after the Second World War?

☐ **A** Canada and India

☐ **B** India and Pakistan

☐ **C** South Africa and Pakistan

☐ **D** South Africa and India

Question 8   Which TWO are famous UK landmarks?

☐ **A** Loch Lomond and Notre Dame

☐ **B** Snowdonia and Notre Dame

☐ **C** Snowdonia and Loch Lomond

☐ **D** Grand Canyon and Loch Lomond

Question 9   Is the statement below ☐ TRUE or ☐ FALSE?

All citizens and permanent residents of the UK can choose which laws they follow.

Question 10 Is the statement below ☐ TRUE or ☐ FALSE?

The House of Lords always acts as the government wishes.

Question 11 Which of the following statements is correct?

☐ **A** Cricket matches can last up to five days.

☐ **B** Cricket matches can last up to two weeks.

Question 12 Is the statement below ☐ TRUE or ☐ FALSE?

The main political parties actively look for members of the public to help at elections and contribute to their costs.

Question 13 What type of government was formed after the General Election of 2010?

☐ **A** National
☐ **B** All-party
☐ **C** One-party
☐ **D** Coalition

Question 14 Is the statement below ☐ TRUE or ☐ FALSE?

In 1707 the kingdoms of England and Scotland were united.

Question 15 Which TWO are political parties in the UK?

☐ **A** Modern Party and Conservative Party
☐ **B** Office Party and Labour Party
☐ **C** Modern Party and Labour Party
☐ **D** Conservative Party and Labour Party

Question 16 Which of the following statements is correct?

☐ **A** The Anglo-Saxon kingdoms in England united under King Alfred the Great.
☐ **B** The Anglo-Saxon kingdoms in England united under King Kenneth MacAlpin.

Question 17 Is the statement below ☐ TRUE or ☐ FALSE?

Wales, Scotland and Northern Ireland each have devolved administrations which give them total control over all policies and laws.

Question 18 Which of the following statements is correct?

☐ **A** Decisions on government policies are made by the monarch.

☐ **B** Decisions on government policies are made by the Prime Minister and cabinet.

Question 19 Which TWO patron saints' days occur in March?

☐ **A** St David and St George

☐ **B** St David and St Patrick

☐ **C** St David and St Andrew

☐ **D** St Patrick and St Andrew

Question 20 Which of the following statements is correct?

☐ **A** All Acts of Parliament are made in the monarch's name.

☐ **B** All Acts of Parliament are made in the Prime Minister's name.

Question 21 St George is the patron saint of which country?

☐ **A** England

☐ **B** Scotland

☐ **C** Wales

☐ **D** Northern Ireland

Question 22 Which area of government policy is the responsibility of the Chancellor of the Exchequer?

☐ **A** Education

☐ **B** Health

☐ **C** Economy

☐ **D** Legal affairs

Question 23 What is the name of the Northern Ireland
Assembly building?

☐ **A** The Houses of Parliament

☐ **B** The Senedd

☐ **C** Stormont

☐ **D** Holyrood House

Question 24 When did the Battle of Hastings take place?

☐ **A** 1066

☐ **B** 1415

☐ **C** 1642

☐ **D** 1940

Answers to Practice Test 11

Question number	Answer	Explanation	Handbook chapter	Handbook page reference
1	A	Sir Steve Redgrave won gold medals in rowing in five consecutive Olympic Games and is one of Britain's greatest Olympians.	A modern, thriving society	Page 85
2	A	The Commonwealth is based on the core values of democracy, good government and the rule of law.	The UK government, the law and your role	Page 137
3	B	Television was developed by John Logie Baird in the 1920s. Tim Berners-Lee invented the World Wide Web in 1990.	A long and illustrious history	Pages 64–5
4	B	The Battle of Britain was fought in the air above Britain in 1940. The British resisted with their fighter planes and eventually won the crucial aerial battle against the Germans, in the summer of 1940.	A long and illustrious history	Page 58
5	B	The devolved administrations in Scotland, Wales and Northern Ireland can pass laws on matters that directly affect them, including health and education.	The UK government, the law and your role	Page 129
6	FALSE	The Home Secretary is the government minister responsible for crime, policing and immigration. The Foreign Secretary is the government minister responsible for managing relationships with foreign countries.	The UK government, the law and your role	Page 127
7	B	Textile and engineering firms from the north of England and the Midlands sent agents to India and Pakistan to find workers.	A long and illustrious history	Page 63

Question number	Answer	Explanation	Handbook chapter	Handbook page reference
8	C	Loch Lomond is the largest expanse of fresh water in mainland Britain and probably the best-known part of the Trossachs National Park. Snowdonia is a national park in North Wales.	A modern, thriving society	Pages 112 and 114
9	FALSE	There are responsibilities and freedoms which are shared by all those living in the UK. These include respecting and obeying the law.	The values and principles of the UK	Page 8
10	FALSE	The House of Lords is normally more independent of the government than the House of Commons.	The UK government, the law and your role	Page 125
11	A	Some cricket games can last for up to five days and still result in a draw.	A modern, thriving society	Page 86
12	TRUE	The main political parties actively look for members of the public to join their debates, contribute to their costs, and help at elections for Parliament or for local government. They have branches in most constituencies and hold policy-making conferences every year.	The UK government, the law and your role	Page 128
13	D	The 2010 coalition was formed by the Conservative and Liberal Democrat parties.	A long and illustrious history	Page 69
14	TRUE	The Act of Union, known as the Treaty of Union in Scotland, was agreed in 1707 and created the Kingdom of Great Britain.	A long and illustrious history	Page 38
15	D	The major political parties in the UK include the Conservative Party, the Labour Party and the Liberal Democrats.	The UK government, the law and your role	Page 128

Question number	Answer	Explanation	Handbook chapter	Handbook page reference
16	A	The Anglo-Saxon kingdoms in England united under King Alfred the Great, who defeated the Vikings.	A long and illustrious history	Page 19
17	FALSE	Some powers have been devolved from central government to give people in Wales, Scotland and Northern Ireland more control over matters that directly affect them. Some policy and laws remain under central UK government control.	The UK government, the law and your role	Page 129
18	B	The monarch has regular meetings with the Prime Minister, and can advise, warn and encourage, but the decisions on government policies are made by the Prime Minister and cabinet.	The UK government, the law and your role	Page 121
19	B	St David, the patron saint of Wales, has a special day on 1 March. St Patrick, the patron saint of Northern Ireland (and Ireland), has a special day on 17 March.	A modern, thriving society	Page 77
20	A	The monarch is the head of state of the UK. All Acts of Parliament are made in the monarch's name.	The UK government, the law and your role	Page 122
21	B	St George is the patron saint of England, and is celebrated on 23rd of April each year.	A modern, thriving society	Page 77
22	C	The Chancellor of the Exchequer is responsible for the economy, and is a member of the cabinet.	The UK government, the law and your role	Page 127
23	C	The Northern Ireland Assembly building is known as Stormont.	The UK government, the law and your role	Page 132

Question number	Answer	Explanation	Handbook chapter	Handbook page reference
24	A	The Battle of Hastings took place in 1066.	A long and illustrious history	Page 19

Practice Test 12

Question 1 What is the title of the National Anthem of the UK?

☐ **A** Long Live the Queen

☐ **B** God Save the Queen

☐ **C** Long Live the Monarch

☐ **D** Almighty is the Queen

Question 2 Is the statement below ☐ TRUE or ☐ FALSE?

In the UK you are expected to treat others with fairness.

Question 3 Where is the Senedd based?

☐ **A** London

☐ **B** Newport

☐ **C** Glasgow

☐ **D** Cardiff

Question 4 Which of the following statements is correct?

☐ **A** There are 50 pence in a pound.

☐ **B** There are 10 pence in a pound.

☐ **C** There are 100 pence in a pound.

☐ **D** There are 20 pence in a pound.

Question 5 Which TWO of the following were English Civil War battles?

☐ **A** Marston Moor and Hastings

☐ **B** Waterloo and Marston Moor

☐ **C** Hastings and Naseby

☐ **D** Marston Moor and Naseby

Question 6 How is the Speaker of the House of Commons chosen?

☐ **A** By the monarch

☐ **B** Through a public election

☐ **C** In a secret ballot

☐ **D** By the Prime Minister

Question 7 Which of the following statements is correct?

☐ **A** The BBC is primarily funded by advertising.

☐ **B** The BBC is partially funded by the state.

Question 8 Which of these groups can take part in the National Citizen Service programme?

☐ **A** All children up to the age of 17

☐ **B** Pensioners

☐ **C** 16- and 17-year-olds

☐ **D** 18- to 30-year-olds

Question 9 Which of the following statements is correct?

☐ **A** The Proms is an eight-week summer season of classical orchestral music.

☐ **B** The Proms is a series of tennis matches held every June in London.

Question 10 Which TWO are influential British bands?

☐ **A** The National Trust and The Rolling Stones

☐ **B** The National Trust and The Beatles

☐ **C** The Rolling Stones and The Beatles

☐ **D** The Rolling Stones and The Royal Family

Question 11   St David is the patron saint of which country of the UK?

☐ **A** England

☐ **B** Scotland

☐ **C** Wales

☐ **D** Northern Ireland

Question 12   The Bill of Rights of 1689 limited whose powers?

☐ **A** The king's

☐ **B** Parliament's

☐ **C** Judges'

☐ **D** The Church's

Question 13   Who elects Police and Crime Commissioners (PCCs)?

☐ **A** The police

☐ **B** The Home Office

☐ **C** The public

☐ **D** Members of Parliament

Question 14   In which part of the British Empire did the Boer War of 1899–1902 take place?

☐ **A** India

☐ **B** Canada

☐ **C** Australia

☐ **D** South Africa

Question 15 Which of the following statements is correct?

☐ **A** The capital city of Northern Ireland is Swansea.

☐ **B** The capital city of Northern Ireland is Belfast.

Question 16 Which TWO of the following issues can the Northern Ireland Assembly make decisions on?

☐ **A** Defence and foreign affairs

☐ **B** Agriculture and social services

☐ **C** Defence and agriculture

☐ **D** Foreign affairs and social services

Question 17 Which of the following statements is correct?

☐ **A** The official home of the Prime Minister is 10 Downing Street.

☐ **B** The official home of the Prime Minister is Buckingham Palace.

Question 18 At what age can you vote in a General Election in the UK?

☐ **A** 16

☐ **B** 18

☐ **C** 21

☐ **D** 23

Question 19 Is the statement below ☐ TRUE or ☐ FALSE?

The flower that is particularly associated with England is the rose.

Question 20 Which of the following statements is correct?

- ☐ **A** The public can listen to debates in the House of Commons.
- ☐ **B** No member of the public is allowed to attend debates in the House of Commons.

Question 21 What was the Beveridge Report of 1942 about?

- ☐ **A** How to end the war in Europe
- ☐ **B** How to treat the Germans and Japanese after the war
- ☐ **C** Establishing a welfare state
- ☐ **D** The coalition government

Question 22 On which date is St Patrick's Day celebrated?

- ☐ **A** 1 March
- ☐ **B** 17 March
- ☐ **C** 23 April
- ☐ **D** 30 November

Question 23 Which of the following statements is correct?

- ☐ **A** The Industrial Revolution is the name given to the rapid development of industry in Britain in the 20th century.
- ☐ **B** The Industrial Revolution is the name given to the rapid development of industry that began in the 18th century.

Question 24 What were TWO important aspects of the Reform Act of 1832?

☐ **A** It abolished rotten boroughs and gave women the vote.

☐ **B** It decreased the power of the monarch and it gave women the vote.

☐ **C** It greatly increased the number of people who could vote and abolished rotten boroughs.

☐ **D** It decreased the power of the monarch and it gave women the vote.

Answers to Practice Test 12

Question number	Answer	Explanation	Handbook chapter	Handbook page reference
1	B	The National Anthem of the UK is 'God Save the Queen'. It is played at important national occasions and at events attended by the Queen or the Royal Family.	The UK government, the law and your role	Page 122
2	TRUE	There are responsibilities and freedoms which are shared by all those living in the UK. These include treating others with fairness.	The values and principles of the UK	Page 8
3	D	The Senedd is based in Cardiff, the capital city of Wales.	The UK government, the law and your role	Page 129
4	C	The currency in the UK is the pound sterling (symbol £). There are 100 pence in a pound.	A long and illustrious history	Page 74
5	D	The Battles of Marston Moor and Naseby were English Civil War battles.	A long and illustrious history	Page 33
6	C	The Speaker is chosen by other Members of Parliament (MPs) in a secret ballot. The Speaker keeps order during political debates to make sure the rules are followed.	The UK government, the law and your role	Page 125
7	B	The BBC is a British public service broadcaster providing television and radio programmes. Although it receives some state funding, it is independent of the government.	A modern, thriving society	Page 106

Question number	Answer	Explanation	Handbook chapter	Handbook page reference
8	C	The National Citizen Service programme gives 16- and 17-year-olds the opportunity to enjoy outdoor activities, develop their skills and take part in a community project.	The UK government, the law and your role	Page 160
9	A	The Proms is an eight-week summer season of orchestral classical music that takes place in various venues, including the Royal Albert Hall in London.	A modern, thriving society	Page 90
10	C	The Beatles and The Rolling Stones are two British bands that continue to have an influence on music both in the UK and abroad.	A modern, thriving society	Page 63
11	C	St David is the patron saint of Wales, and St David's Day is celebrated on 1 March each year.	A modern, thriving society	Page 77
12	A	The Bill of Rights of 1689 confirmed the rights of Parliament and the limits of the king's power.	A long and illustrious history	Page 37
13	C	The public elects Police and Crime Commissioners (PCCs) in England and Wales. PCCs are responsible for the delivery of an efficient and effective police force.	The UK government, the law and your role	Page 142
14	D	The Boer War took place in South Africa between the British army and the Boer settlers, who originally came from the Netherlands.	A long and illustrious history	Page 51
15	B	The capital city of Northern Ireland is Belfast.	A modern, thriving society	Page 72
16	B	The Northern Ireland Assembly can make decisions on various issues, including agriculture and social services.	The UK government, the law and your role	Page 132

Question number	Answer	Explanation	Handbook chapter	Handbook page reference
17	A	The official home of the Prime Minister is 10 Downing Street, in central London, near the Houses of Parliament. He or she also has a country house outside London called Chequers.	The UK government, the law and your role	Page 127
18	B	The present voting age of 18 was set in 1969.	The UK government, the law and your role	Page 120
19	TRUE	The countries that make up the UK all have flowers which are particularly associated with them and which are sometimes worn on national saints' days. In England, the flower is the rose.	A modern, thriving society	Page 101
20	A	The public can listen to debates from public galleries in both the House of Commons and the House of Lords.	The UK government, the law and your role	Page 135
21	C	The Beveridge Report of 1942, called Social Insurance and Allied Services, recommended that the government should find ways of fighting the five 'Giant Evils' of Want, Disease, Ignorance, Squalor and Idleness and provided the basis of the modern welfare state.	A long and illustrious history	Page 62
22	B	St Patrick, the patron saint of Northern Ireland (and Ireland), has a special day on 17 March.	A modern, thriving society	Page 77
23	B	The Industrial Revolution refers to the rapid development of industry in Britain from the mid-18th century.	A long and illustrious history	Page 40

Question number	Answer	Explanation	Handbook chapter	Handbook page reference
24	C	The Reform Act of 1832 greatly increased the number of people with the right to vote. The Act also abolished the old pocket and rotten boroughs (parliamentary seats where there were few voters) and more parliamentary seats were given to the towns and cities.	A long and illustrious history	Page 50

Practice Test 13

Question 1   Which TWO rights are offered by the UK to citizens and permanent residents?

☐ **A** Free groceries for everyone and a right to a fair trial

☐ **B** Long lunch breaks on Friday and a right to a fair trial

☐ **C** Freedom of speech and a right to a fair trial

☐ **D** Freedom of speech and free groceries for everyone

Question 2   Which of the following statements is correct?

☐ **A** The small claims procedure is an informal way of helping people to settle minor disputes.

☐ **B** The small claims procedure helps people to make small home insurance claims.

Question 3   Which of the following is the capital city of Wales?

☐ **A** Swansea

☐ **B** Cardiff

☐ **C** Edinburgh

☐ **D** Belfast

Question 4   Which of the following statements is correct?

☐ **A** It is free to visit the Houses of Parliament to listen to debates.

☐ **B** It costs £15 per person to visit the Houses of Parliament to listen to debates.

Question 5   Is the statement below ☐ TRUE or ☐ FALSE?

The 'Swinging Sixties' is a reference to the 1860s.

Question 6 Which of the following statements is correct?

☐ **A** The official Church of state in England is the Church of England.

☐ **B** There is no official Church of state in England.

Question 7 Which TWO of the following plants are particularly associated with the UK?

☐ **A** Shamrock and rose

☐ **B** Cactus and olive tree

☐ **C** Rose and cactus

☐ **D** Shamrock and cactus

Question 8 Which of the following statements is correct?

☐ **A** 'The Divine Right of Kings' was the idea that the English king should rule France.

☐ **B** 'The Divine Right of Kings' was the idea that the king was directly appointed by God to rule.

Question 9 Which TWO records tell us about England during the time of William the Conqueror?

☐ **A** The Domesday Book and the Bayeux Tapestry

☐ **B** The Diary of Samuel Pepys and the Bayeux Tapestry

☐ **C** The Domesday Book and the Magna Carta

☐ **D** The Diary of Samuel Pepys and the Magna Carta

Question 10 Which of the following statements is correct?

☐ **A** Police and Crime Commissioners (PCCs) are appointed through a public election.

☐ **B** Police and Crime Commissioners (PCCs) are appointed by the local council.

Question 11 What is the name of the UK currency?

☐ **A** Dollar

☐ **B** Euro

☐ **C** Pound sterling

☐ **D** Yen

Question 12 Which TWO of the following were introduced in the early 20th century?

☐ **A** Child Benefit payments and free school meals

☐ **B** The National Health Service (NHS) and Child Benefit payments

☐ **C** The National Health Service (NHS) and old-age pensions

☐ **D** Old-age pensions and free school meals

Question 13 Who opens the new parliamentary session each year?

☐ **A** The Archbishop of Canterbury

☐ **B** The Prime Minister

☐ **C** The Speaker of the House of Commons

☐ **D** The Queen

Question 14 Is the statement below ☐ TRUE or ☐ FALSE?

The Scottish Parliament can pass laws for Scotland on all matters.

Question 15 Which of the following statements is correct?

☐ **A** The Queen is ceremonial head of the Commonwealth.

☐ **B** The Queen is ceremonial head of the North Atlantic Treaty Organization (NATO).

Question 16 Which significant change was introduced by the Education Act of 1944?

☐ **A** New public examinations

☐ **B** Free secondary education in England and Wales

☐ **C** Primary education for all

☐ **D** The requirement to wear school uniform

Question 17 Which of the following is a responsibility you will have as a citizen or permanent resident of the UK?

☐ **A** To keep your dog on a lead at all times

☐ **B** To avoid shopping on a Sunday

☐ **C** To look after yourself and your family

☐ **D** To grow your own vegetables.

Question 18 Which of the following statements is correct?

☐ **A** Hadrian's Wall was built by the Roman Emperor Hadrian.

☐ **B** Hadrian's Wall was built by the Picts (ancestors of the Scottish people) to keep out the Romans.

Question 19 Is the statement below ☐ TRUE OR ☐ FALSE?

The National Citizen Service provides military training to young people.

Question 20 In everyday language, people may say 'rain stopped play'. With which sport is this phrase associated?

☐ **A** Football
☐ **B** Cricket
☐ **C** Rugby league
☐ **D** Horse racing

Question 21 Which of the following statements is correct?

☐ **A** The Battle of Agincourt is commemorated in the Bayeux Tapestry.
☐ **B** The Battle of Hastings is commemorated in the Bayeux Tapestry.

Question 22 Which cross on the Union Flag represents the patron saint of Scotland?

☐ **A** The diagonal white cross
☐ **B** The diagonal red cross
☐ **C** The upright red cross
☐ **D** None of these

Question 23 Which TWO of the following are linked to football?

☐ **A** The Premier League and The Open
☐ **B** UEFA and the Premier League
☐ **C** The Ashes and UEFA
☐ **D** The Ashes and The Open

Question 24 Is the statement below ☐ TRUE or ☐ FALSE?

The Lake District is England's largest national park.

Answers to Practice Test 13

Question number	Answer	Explanation	Handbook chapter	Handbook page reference
1	C	There are responsibilities and freedoms which are shared by all those living in the UK. These include freedom of speech and a right to a fair trial.	The values and principles of the UK	Page 8
2	A	The small claims procedure is an informal way of helping people to settle minor disputes without spending a lot of time and money using a lawyer.	The UK government, the law and your role	Page 147
3	B	The capital city of Wales is Cardiff.	A modern, thriving society	Page 72
4	A	The public can listen to debates from public galleries in both the House of Commons and the House of Lords. Entrance is free. You can write to your local MP in advance to ask for tickets or you can queue on the day at the public entrance.	The UK government, the law and your role	Page 135
5	FALSE	The decade of the 1960s was a period of significant social change. It was known as 'the Swinging Sixties'. There was growth in British fashion, cinema and popular music.	A long and illustrious history	Page 63
6	A	The Church of England is the official Church of state in England. The monarch is the head of the Church of England.	A modern, thriving society	Page 77
7	A	The countries that make up the UK all have flowers which are particularly associated with them and which are sometimes worn on national saints' days. In England, the flower is the rose; in Northern Ireland it is the shamrock.	A modern, thriving society	Page 101

Question number	Answer	Explanation	Handbook chapter	Handbook page reference
8	B	The 'Divine Right of Kings' was the idea that the king was directly appointed by God to rule.	A long and illustrious history	Page 32
9	A	The Domesday Book is a record of towns and villages in England. The Bayeux Tapestry tells the story of the Norman Conquest.	A long and illustrious history	Pages 19–20
10	A	The public in England and Wales elect Police and Crime Commissioners (PCCs). The first elections for PCCs were held in November 2012.	The UK government, the law and your role	Page 142
11	C	The currency in the UK is the pound sterling (symbol £). There are 100 pence in a pound.	A modern, thriving society	Page 74
12	D	The early 20th century was a time of social progress. Old-age pensions and free school meals were just a few of the important measures introduced.	A long and illustrious history	Page 53
13	D	The Queen has important ceremonial roles, such as the opening of the new parliamentary session each year.	The UK government, the law and your role	Page 121
14	FALSE	The Scottish Parliament can pass laws for Scotland on all matters that are not specifically reserved to the UK Parliament.	The UK government, the law and your role	Page 131
15	A	The Queen is the ceremonial head of the Commonwealth, which currently has 54 member states.	The UK government, the law and your role	Page 137
16	B	The Education Act of 1944 (often called 'The Butler Act' after the Minister of Education at the time, R A Butler) introduced free secondary education in England and Wales.	A long and illustrious history	Page 62

Question number	Answer	Explanation	Handbook chapter	Handbook page reference
17	C	There are responsibilities and freedoms which are shared by all those living in the UK. These include looking after yourself and your family.	The values and principles of the UK	Page 8
18	A	The Emperor Hadrian built a wall in the north of England (Hadrian's Wall) to keep out the Picts (ancestors of the Scottish people).	A long and illustrious history	Page 17
19	FALSE	The National Citizen Service gives 16- and 17-year-olds the opportunity to enjoy outdoor activities, develop their skills and take part in a community project.	The UK government, the law and your role	Page 160
20	B	The expression 'rain stopped play' is associated with cricket. The phrase has now passed into everyday usage.	A modern, thriving society	Page 86
21	B	The Bayeux Tapestry commemorates the victory of William, Duke of Normandy at the Battle of Hastings in 1066.	A long and illustrious history	Page 19
22	A	The cross of St Andrew, patron saint of Scotland, is a diagonal white cross on a blue ground.	A long and illustrious history	Page 45
23	B	The English Premier League attracts a huge international audience. Many of the best players in the world play in the Premier League. Many UK teams also compete in competitions such as the UEFA (Union of European Football Associations) Champions League, against other teams from Europe.	A modern, thriving society	Page 87
24	TRUE	The Lake District is England's largest national park. It covers 912 square miles (2,362 square kilometres).	A modern, thriving society	Page 116

Practice Test 14

Question 1   Which of the following statements is correct?

☐ **A** The Reform Act of 1832 greatly increased the number of people who had the right to vote.

☐ **B** The Reform Act of 1832 increased the power of the House of Lords.

Question 2   Which cross on the Union Flag represents the patron saint of Ireland?

☐ **A** The diagonal white cross

☐ **B** The diagonal red cross

☐ **C** The upright red cross

☐ **D** None of these

Question 3   Which of the following statements is correct?

☐ **A** The capital cities of the nations of the UK are London, Swansea, Glasgow and Dublin.

☐ **B** The capital cities of the nations of the UK are London, Cardiff, Edinburgh and Belfast.

Question 4   Which Scottish king defeated the English at the Battle of Bannockburn in 1314?

☐ **A** William Wallace

☐ **B** Robert the Bruce

☐ **C** Malcolm

☐ **D** Andrew

Question 5 Which TWO points about slavery are correct?

☐ **A** William Wilberforce was a leading abolitionist and the Royal Navy refused to stop ships carrying slaves.

☐ **B** Quakers set up the first anti-slavery groups and the Royal Navy refused to stop ships carrying slaves.

☐ **C** Slavery survived in the British Empire until the early 20th century and the Royal Navy refused to stop ships carrying slaves.

☐ **D** William Wilberforce was a leading abolitionist and Quakers set up the first anti-slavery groups.

Question 6 Is the statement below ☐ TRUE or ☐ FALSE?

The daffodil is the national flower of Wales.

Question 7 Is the statement below ☐ TRUE or ☐ FALSE?

The First World War ended at 11.00 am on 11 November 1918.

Question 8 Where do the Laurence Olivier awards take place?

☐ **A** London

☐ **B** Cardiff

☐ **C** Edinburgh

☐ **D** Belfast

Question 9 Which of the following statements is correct?

☐ **A** The Speaker of the House of Commons remains a Member of Parliament (MP) after election as Speaker.

☐ **A** The Speaker of the House of Commons has to give up being an MP when elected as Speaker.

Question 10 Which sport can be traced back to 15th-century Scotland?

- ☐ **A** Surfing
- ☐ **B** Formula 1
- ☐ **C** Golf
- ☐ **D** Motorbike racing

Question 11 Why was the Habeas Corpus Act of 1679 so important?

- ☐ **A** It ensured no person could be held prisoner unlawfully.
- ☐ **B** It allowed people to bury the dead where they wished.
- ☐ **C** It ensured that those who died could only be buried by a relative.
- ☐ **D** It ended capital punishment in England.

Question 12 Is the statement below ☐ TRUE or ☐ FALSE?

The British Broadcasting Corporation (BBC) is financed by income tax.

Question 13 What system of government does the UK have?

- ☐ **A** Communist government
- ☐ **B** Dictatorship
- ☐ **C** Parliamentary democracy
- ☐ **D** Federal government

Question 14 Which of the following statements is correct?

- ☐ **A** The Highland Clearances took place in Scotland.
- ☐ **B** The Highland Clearances took place in Ireland.

Question 15 Which TWO responsibilities do you have as a resident of the UK?

☐ **A** Respect and obey the law, and take in and look after wild animals.

☐ **B** Treat others with fairness and vote for the government in power.

☐ **C** Treat others with fairness, and take in and look after wild animals.

☐ **D** Respect and obey the law and treat others with fairness.

Question 16 Which of the following statements is correct?

☐ **A** A free press means that what is written in newspapers is free from government control.

☐ **B** A free press means that newspapers are given out free of charge.

Question 17 To which TWO international associations or agreements does the UK belong?

☐ **A** The North Atlantic Treaty Organization (NATO) and the North American Free Trade Agreement (NAFTA)

☐ **B** The North Atlantic Treaty Organization (NATO) and the Commonwealth

☐ **C** The Commonwealth and the Arab League

☐ **D** The Commonwealth and the North American Free Trade Agreement (NAFTA)

Question 18 Which of the following statements is correct?

☐ **A** *The Mousetrap* is a play that has been running in London's West End since 1952.

☐ **B** *The Mousetrap* is an environmental policy aiming to prevent mice from destroying crops.

Question 19 Which TWO were 20th-century British discoveries or inventions?

☐ **A** Radium and the printing press

☐ **B** The hovercraft and radium

☐ **C** Penicillin and the printing press

☐ **D** The hovercraft and penicillin

Question 20 Which of the following statements is correct?

☐ **A** The National Trust is a charity that works to preserve important buildings in the UK.

☐ **B** The National Trust is a government-run organisation that provides funding for charities.

Question 21 Which of the following statements is correct?

☐ **A** The Industrial Revolution was the rapid development of industry in the 18th and 19th centuries.

☐ **B** The Industrial Revolution introduced changes in the banking system in the 1970s.

Question 22 Is the statement below ☐ TRUE or ☐ FALSE?

St Helena is a Crown dependency.

Question 23 Which of the following is part of the UK?

☐ **A** The Channel Islands

☐ **B** Northern Ireland

☐ **C** The Isle of Man

☐ **D** The Falkland Islands

Question 24 Which of the following do you need to do in order to get a full driving licence?

☐ **A** Pass a driving test

☐ **B** Buy a car or van

☐ **C** Pay income tax

☐ **D** Find a full-time job

Answers to Practice Test 14

Question number	Answer	Explanation	Handbook chapter	Handbook page reference
1	A	The Reform Act of 1832 greatly increased the number of people with the right to vote. The Act also abolished the old pocket and rotten boroughs (parliamentary seats where there were few voters) and more parliamentary seats were given to the towns and cities.	A long and illustrious history	Page 50
2	B	The cross of St Patrick, patron saint of Ireland, is a diagonal red cross on a white background.	A long and illustrious history	Page 45
3	B	The capital cities of the nations of the UK are: London (England), Cardiff (Wales), Edinburgh (Scotland) and Belfast (Northern Ireland).	A modern, thriving society	Page 72
4	B	The English were defeated at the Battle of Bannockburn by Robert the Bruce in 1314.	A long and illustrious history	Page 21
5	D	The first formal anti-slavery groups were set up by the Quakers in the late 1700s, and they petitioned Parliament to ban the practice. William Wilberforce, an evangelical Christian and a Member of Parliament, also played an important part in changing the law, and in 1833 the Emancipation Act abolished slavery throughout the British Empire.	A long and illustrious history	Page 43
6	TRUE	The daffodil is the national flower of Wales, and is worn on St David's Day.	A modern, thriving society	Page 101

Question number	Answer	Explanation	Handbook chapter	Handbook page reference
7	TRUE	The First World War ended at 11.00 am on 11th November 1918 with victory for Britain and its allies.	A long and illustrious history	Page 55
8	A	The Laurence Olivier Awards take place annually at different venues in London. There are a variety of categories, including best director, best actor and best actress.	A modern, thriving society	Page 93
9	A	The Speaker is neutral and does not represent a political party, but he or she remains an MP, represents a constituency and deals with constituents' problems like any other MP.	The UK government, the law and your role	Page 125
10	C	The modern game of golf can be traced back to 15th century Scotland.	A modern, thriving society	Page 88
11	A	The Habeas Corpus Act was a very important piece of legislation which remains relevant today. Habeas corpus is Latin for 'you must present the person in court'. The Act guaranteed that no one could be held prisoner unlawfully.	A long and illustrious history	Page 35
12	FALSE	The money from TV licences is used to pay for the British Broadcasting Corporation (BBC). Everyone in the UK with a TV, computer or other medium which can be used for watching TV must have a television licence.	A modern, thriving society	Page 105
13	C	The system of government in the UK is a parliamentary democracy. The UK is divided into parliamentary constituencies, and voters in each constituency elect a Member of Parliament (MP) to represent them.	The UK government, the law and your role	Page 124

Question number	Answer	Explanation	Handbook chapter	Handbook page reference
14	A	The Highland Clearances took place in Scotland. Many Scottish landlords destroyed individual small farms (known as 'crofts') to make space for large flocks of sheep and cattle.	A long and illustrious history	Page 39
15	D	There are responsibilities and freedoms which are shared by all those living in the UK. These include respecting and obeying the law, and treating others with fairness.	The values and principles of the UK	Page 8
16	A	The UK has a free press. This means that what is written in newspapers is free from government control.	The UK government, the law and your role	Page 133
17	B	The UK belongs to many International bodies including NATO (North Atlantic Treaty Organization) and the Commonwealth.	The UK government, the law and your role	Pages 137 and 139
18	A	*The Mousetrap*, a murder-mystery play by Dame Agatha Christie, has been running in the West End since 1952.	A modern, thriving society	Page 93
19	D	The hovercraft was invented by Sir Christopher Cockerell and penicillin was discovered by Sir Alexander Fleming.	A long and illustrious history	Pages 60 and 65
20	A	The National Trust in England, Wales and Northern Ireland, and the National Trust for Scotland, work to preserve important buildings, coastline and countryside.	A modern, thriving society	Page 107

Question number	Answer	Explanation	Handbook chapter	Handbook page reference
21	A	The Industrial Revolution was the rapid development of industry in Britain in the 18th and 19th centuries. The development of machinery and use of steam power transformed industries such as manufacturing and mining.	A long and illustrious history	Page 40
22	FALSE	St Helena is a British overseas territory and not a Crown dependency.	What is the UK?	Page 13
23	B	Northern Ireland is part of the UK, along with England, Wales and Scotland.	What is the UK?	Page 13
24	A	To get a full UK driving licence, you must pass a driving test, which tests both your knowledge and your practical skills.	The UK government, the law and your role	Page 152

Practice Test 15

Question 1 Which cross on the Union Flag represents the patron saint of England?

☐ **A** The diagonal white cross

☐ **B** The diagonal red cross

☐ **C** The upright red cross

☐ **D** None of these

Question 2 What is the aim of the United Nations?

☐ **A** To create a single free trade market

☐ **B** To prevent war and promote international peace and security

☐ **C** To examine decisions made by the European Union

☐ **D** To promote dictatorship

Question 3 Which of the following statements is correct?

☐ **A** The capital city of Scotland is Edinburgh.

☐ **B** The capital city of Scotland is Glasgow.

Question 4 What was the name given to supporters of King Charles I during the Civil War?

☐ **A** Luddites

☐ **B** Roundheads

☐ **C** Cavaliers

☐ **D** Levellers

Question 5 Which season of orchestral classical music has been organised by the BBC since 1927?

- ☐ **A** The Eisteddfod
- ☐ **B** Aldeburgh Festival
- ☐ **C** The Proms
- ☐ **D** Glastonbury

Question 6 Which TWO chambers form the UK Parliament?

- ☐ **A** House of Lords and House of Representatives
- ☐ **B** House of Fraser and House of Commons
- ☐ **C** House of Commons and House of Representatives
- ☐ **D** House of Lords and House of Commons

Question 7 Is the statement below ☐ TRUE or ☐ FALSE?

The shamrock is the national flower of Scotland.

Question 8 To apply for UK citizenship or permanent residency, which TWO things do you need?

- ☐ **A** An ability to speak and read English, and a good knowledge of life in the UK
- ☐ **B** A UK bank account and an ability to speak and read English
- ☐ **C** A UK bank account and a good understanding of life in the UK
- ☐ **D** An ability to speak and read English, and a driving licence

Question 9   Which of the following statements is correct?

☐ **A** There are a few Members of Parliament who do not represent any of the main political parties.

☐ **B** All Members of Parliament have to belong to a political party.

Question 10   Which TWO of the following were major welfare changes introduced from 1945 to 1950?

☐ **A** The National Health Service (NHS) and a national system of benefits

☐ **B** The State retirement pension and employment exchanges

☐ **C** The National Health Service (NHS) and employment exchanges

☐ **D** Employment exchanges and free school meals

Question 11   Which language was spoken by people during the Iron Age?

☐ **A** Latin

☐ **B** A language that was part of the Celtic family

☐ **C** English

☐ **D** Anglo-Saxon

Question 12   Which TWO of the following are part of the UK government?

☐ **A** The cabinet and the civil service

☐ **B** The civil service and FIFA

☐ **C** The National Trust and FIFA

☐ **D** The cabinet and the National Trust

Question 13 Who first built the Tower of London?

☐ **A** Oliver Cromwell

☐ **B** Queen Elizabeth II

☐ **C** William the Conqueror

☐ **D** Winston Churchill

Question 14 Is the statement below ☐ TRUE or ☐ FALSE?

The criminal court systems in England, Wales, Scotland and Northern Ireland are identical.

Question 15 Is the statement below ☐ TRUE or ☐ FALSE?

The Wimbledon Championships are associated with motor sports.

Question 16 Which of the following statements is correct?

☐ **A** By the middle of the 17th century the last Welsh rebellions had been defeated.

☐ **B** By the middle of the 15th century the last Welsh rebellions had been defeated.

Question 17 Is the statement below ☐ TRUE or ☐ FALSE?

There are many variations in language in the different parts of the UK.

Question 18 Is the statement below ☐ TRUE or ☐ FALSE?

The Scottish Parliament sits in Edinburgh.

Question 19 Is the statement below ☐ TRUE or ☐ FALSE?

The jet engine and radar were developed in Britain in the 1830s.

Question 20 What must you do in order to vote in elections?

☐ **A** Pay income tax in the year before the election.

☐ **B** Put your name on the electoral register.

☐ **C** Register your identity with the police.

☐ **D** Pass an electoral test.

Question 21 In which period of British history did people live in roundhouses and bury their dead in tombs called round barrows?

☐ **A** The Middle Ages

☐ **B** The Bronze Age

☐ **C** The Stone Age

☐ **D** The Victorian Age

Question 22 Which of the following statements is correct?

☐ **A** The UK is a member of NATO.

☐ **B** The UK has never been a member of NATO.

Question 23 Which of the following statements is correct?

☐ **A** The Roman army left England after 100 years to defend other parts of their Empire.

☐ **B** The Roman army left England after 400 years to defend other parts of their Empire.

Question 24 Which of the following is a British overseas territory?

☐ **A** Northern Ireland

☐ **B** Falkland Islands

☐ **C** France

☐ **D** USA

Answers to Practice Test 15

Question number	Answer	Explanation	Handbook chapter	Handbook page reference
1	C	The cross of St George, patron saint of England, is an upright red cross on a white ground.	A long and illustrious history	Page 45
2	B	The UK is part of the United Nations (UN), an international organisation with more than 190 countries as members. The UN was set up after the Second World War and aims to prevent war and promote international peace and security.	The UK government, the law and your role	Page 139
3	A	The capital city of Scotland is Edinburgh.	A modern, thriving society	Page 72
4	C	The king's supporters during the Civil War were called Cavaliers. Those who supported Parliament were called Roundheads.	A long and illustrious history	Page 33
5	C	The Proms is an eight-week summer season of orchestral classical music that takes place in various venues, including the Royal Albert Hall in London. It has been organised by the British Broadcasting Corporation (BBC) since 1927.	A modern, thriving society	Page 90
6	D	The UK Parliament is formed by the House of Commons and the House of Lords.	The UK government, the law and your role	Page 120
7	FALSE	The shamrock is the national flower of Northern Ireland, and the thistle is the national flower of Scotland.	A modern, thriving society	Page 101

Question number	Answer	Explanation	Handbook chapter	Handbook page reference
8	A	To apply to become a permanent resident or a naturalised citizen of the UK, you must be able to speak and read English and have a good understanding of life in the UK.	The values and principles of the UK	Page 9
9	A	There are a few Members of Parliament (MPs) who do not represent any of the main political parties. They are called 'independents'.	The UK government, the law and your role	Page 128
10	A	The Labour government that was elected in 1945 established the National Health Service (NHS) and a national system of benefits.	A long and illustrious history	Page 60
11	B	The language Iron Age people spoke was part of the Celtic language family.	A long and illustrious history	Page 16
12	A	There are several different parts of government in the UK, including the cabinet and the civil service.	The UK government, the law and your role	Page 120
13	C	The Tower of London was first built by William the Conqueror after he became king in 1066.	A modern, thriving society	Page 115
14	FALSE	There are some differences between the criminal court systems in different parts of the UK.	The UK government, the law and your role	Page 144
15	FALSE	The Wimbledon Championships is the oldest tennis tournament in the world.	A modern, thriving society	Page 89
16	B	The last Welsh rebellions were defeated by the middle of the 15th century.	A long and illustrious history	Page 21

Question number	Answer	Explanation	Handbook chapter	Handbook page reference
17	TRUE	There are many variations in language in the different parts of the UK. The English language has many accents and dialects. In Wales, many people speak Welsh. In Scotland, Gaelic is spoken in some parts of the Highlands and Islands, and in Northern Ireland some people speak Irish Gaelic.	A modern, thriving society	Page 74
18	TRUE	The Scottish Parliament was formed in 1999. It sits in Edinburgh, the capital city of Scotland.	The UK government, the law and your role	Page 130
19	FALSE	The jet engine and the radar were both developed in Britain in the 1930s.	A long and illustrious history	Pages 64–5
20	B	To be able to vote in a parliamentary or local election, you must have your name on the electoral register. You can register by contacting your local council electoral registration office.	The UK government, the law and your role	Page 134
21	B	Around 4,000 years ago, people learned to make bronze. We call this period the Bronze Age. People lived in roundhouses and buried their dead in tombs called round barrows.	A long and illustrious history	Page 16
22	A	The UK is a member of NATO (North Atlantic Treaty Organization). NATO is a group of European and North American countries that have agreed to help each other if they come under attack. It also aims to maintain peace between all of its members.	The UK government, the law and your role	Page 139
23	B	The Romans left England in AD 410 to defend other parts of their Empire. They had remained in Britain for 400 years.	A long and illustrious history	Page 17

Question number	Answer	Explanation	Handbook chapter	Handbook page reference
24	B	There are several British overseas territories in other parts of the world, such as the Falkland Islands.	What is the UK?	Page 13

Practice Test 16

Question 1   Which of the following statements is correct?

☐ **A** Wales and Northern Ireland each have their own Church of state.

☐ **B** There is no established Church in Wales or Northern Ireland.

Question 2   Is the statement below ☐ TRUE or ☐ FALSE?

Thomas Hardy was a famous author who wrote *Far from the Madding Crowd*.

Question 3   What was the Reformation?

☐ **A** A reduction in the power of the nobles

☐ **B** A movement against the authority of the Pope

☐ **C** A part of the Wars of the Roses

☐ **D** A bill of rights

Question 4   Which of the following statements is correct?

☐ **A** In the UK, pregnant women have the same right to work as anyone else.

☐ **B** In the UK, employers have the right not to employ pregnant women.

Question 5   Hadrian's Wall was built to keep out whom?

☐ **A** The Irish

☐ **B** The Welsh

☐ **C** The Picts

☐ **D** The Vikings

Question 6 Where did the Vikings come from?

☐ **A** Germany and Austria

☐ **B** Belgium and Holland

☐ **C** Denmark, Norway and Sweden

☐ **D** France and Luxembourg

Question 7 Which of the following statements is correct?

☐ **A** Volunteering is a good way to earn additional money.

☐ **B** Volunteering is a way of helping others without receiving payment.

Question 8 Is the statement below ☐ TRUE or ☐ FALSE?

People can see the Crown Jewels at the Tower of London.

Question 9 For which TWO types of literature is William Shakespeare famous?

☐ **A** Plays and sonnets

☐ **B** Biographies and sonnets

☐ **C** Novels and biographies

☐ **D** Novels and plays

Question 10 For which TWO reasons is Henry VIII remembered?

☐ **A** Married six times and fought in the Battle of Agincourt

☐ **B** Married six times and broke away from the Church of Rome

☐ **C** Introduced the game of croquet and married six times

☐ **D** Introduced the game of croquet and fought in the Battle of Agincourt

Question 11 For approximately how many years did the Romans remain in Britain?

☐ **A** 50 years

☐ **B** 100 years

☐ **C** 400 years

☐ **D** 600 years

Question 12 Is the statement below ☐ TRUE or ☐ FALSE?

UK population growth has been faster in more recent years.

Question 13 Which of the following statements is correct?

☐ **A** When buying a car, you must pay an annual vehicle tax.

☐ **B** When buying a car, you do not need to pay vehicle tax if the previous owner has already paid it.

Question 14 The Union Flag consists of three crosses. One is the cross of St George. Who do the other TWO crosses represent?

- ☐ **A** St David and St Piran
- ☐ **B** St David and St Andrew
- ☐ **C** St Patrick and St Andrew
- ☐ **D** St Patrick and St Piran

Question 15 Which of the following statements is correct?

- ☐ **A** Charles, king of Scotland, was crowned King Charles II of England in 1660.
- ☐ **B** Bonnie Prince Charlie became King Charles II of England in 1660.

Question 16 Which TWO of the following types of case are held in County Courts?

- ☐ **A** Divorce and murder
- ☐ **B** Murder and minor criminal offences
- ☐ **C** Minor criminal offences and breaches of contract
- ☐ **D** Divorce and breaches of contract

Question 17 Which of the following is a famous landmark in Wales?

- ☐ **A** Snowdon
- ☐ **B** Loch Lomond
- ☐ **C** Windermere
- ☐ **D** The Giant's Causeway

Question 18 What celebration takes place each year on
14 February?

☐ **A** Valentine's Day
☐ **B** Bonfire Night
☐ **C** Halloween
☐ **D** Hogmanay

Question 19 Which TWO of the following were British inventions?

☐ **A** Television and the jet engine
☐ **B** The jet engine and radio
☐ **C** Television and the diesel engine
☐ **D** Radio and the diesel engine

Question 20 Henry VII established the House of Tudor. What
colour rose became the Tudor emblem?

☐ **A** White
☐ **B** Red and white
☐ **C** Red
☐ **D** Pink

Question 21 Which countries make up 'Great Britain'?

☐ **A** Just England
☐ **B** England, Scotland and Wales
☐ **C** England and Scotland
☐ **D** England, Scotland and Northern Ireland

Question 22 Which TWO of the following are traditional British foods?

- ☐ **A** Strudel and haggis
- ☐ **B** Welsh cakes and haggis
- ☐ **C** Sushi and Welsh cakes
- ☐ **D** Sushi and haggis

Question 23 Which of the following is the capital city of the UK?

- ☐ **A** Westminster
- ☐ **B** Birmingham
- ☐ **C** Windsor
- ☐ **D** London

Question 24 Which of the following is a Crown dependency?

- ☐ **A** England
- ☐ **B** Northern Ireland
- ☐ **C** Channel Islands
- ☐ **D** Scotland

Answers to Practice Test 16

Question number	Answer	Explanation	Handbook chapter	Handbook page reference
1	B	There is no established Church in Wales or Northern Ireland.	A modern, thriving society	Page 77
2	TRUE	Thomas Hardy (1840–1928) was an author and poet. His best-known novels focus on rural society and include *Far from the Madding Crowd* and *Jude the Obscure*.	A modern, thriving society	Page 98
3	B	The Reformation occurred across Europe. It was a movement against the authority of the Pope and the ideas and practices of the Roman Catholic Church.	A long and illustrious history	Page 27
4	A	UK laws ensure people are not treated unfairly in any area of life or work because of their age, disability, sex, pregnancy and maternity, race, religion or belief, sexuality or marital status.	The UK government, the law and your role	Page 149
5	C	The Roman Emperor Hadrian built the wall in the north of England to keep out the Picts (ancestors of the Scottish people).	A long and illustrious history	Page 17
6	C	The Vikings first raided Britain in AD 789. They came from Denmark, Norway and Sweden.	A long and illustrious history	Page 19
7	B	Volunteering is working for good causes without payment. There are many activities you can do as a volunteer, such as working with the homeless and helping improve the environment.	The UK government, the law and your role	Page 158
8	TRUE	People can see the Crown Jewels at the Tower of London.	A modern, thriving society	Page 115

Question number	Answer	Explanation	Handbook chapter	Handbook page reference
9	A	William Shakespeare was a famous playwright and sonnet writer.	A modern, thriving society	Page 99
10	B	Henry VIII is remembered for breaking away from the Catholic Church of Rome and marrying six times.	A long and illustrious history	Page 26
11	C	The Romans remained in Britain for almost 400 years, from AD 43 to AD 410.	A long and illustrious history	Page 17
12	TRUE	UK population growth has been faster in more recent years. Migration into the UK and longer life expectancy have played a part in this.	A modern, thriving society	Page 75
13	A	When you buy a car, you must pay an annual vehicle tax, which cannot be passed on when a vehicle changes hands.	The UK government, the law and your role	Page 153
14	C	The Union Flag consists of the crosses of Saints George, Andrew and Patrick.	A long and illustrious history	Page 45
15	A	The Scots declared Charles II to be king. He was crowned king of Scotland and led a Scottish army into England. After defeat at the Battles of Dunbar and Worcester, he fled to Europe. In May 1660, Parliament invited him to come back from exile in the Netherlands. He was crowned King Charles II of England, Wales, Scotland and Ireland.	A long and illustrious history	Page 34
16	D	County Courts deal with a wide range of civil disputes, including divorce and other family matters, and breaches of contract.	The UK government, the law and your role	Page 146
17	A	Snowdonia is a national park in North Wales. Its most well-known landmark is Snowdon, which is the highest mountain in Wales.	A modern, thriving society	Page 114

Question number	Answer	Explanation	Handbook chapter	Handbook page reference
18	A	Valentine's Day, on 14 February, is when lovers exchange cards and gifts. Sometimes people send anonymous cards to someone they secretly admire.	A modern, thriving society	Page 82
19	A	The television and jet engine are two of many important inventions by Britons in the 20th century.	A long and illustrious history	Pages 64–5
20	B	The Tudor rose was a red rose with a white rose inside it, showing the alliance between the Houses of York and Lancaster, which had previously fought against each other.	A long and illustrious history	Page 25
21	B	'Great Britain' refers only to England, Scotland and Wales, not to Northern Ireland. The official name of the country is the United Kingdom of Great Britain and Northern Ireland.	What is the UK?	Page 13
22	B	Welsh cakes are a traditional Welsh snack made from flour, dried fruits and spices. Haggis, a traditional Scottish food, is a sheep's stomach stuffed with offal, suet, onions and oatmeal.	A modern, thriving society	Page 102
23	D	The capital city of the UK is London, which is in England.	A modern, thriving society	Page 72
24	C	The Channel Islands are closely linked with the UK but are not part of it. These islands have their own governments and are called 'Crown dependencies'.	What is the UK?	Page 13

Practice Test 17

Question 1   Is the statement below ☐ TRUE or ☐ FALSE?

*The Union Flag consists of four crosses, one
for each part of the United Kingdom.*

Question 2   Which of the following statements is correct?

☐ **A** To apply to become a permanent resident or
naturalised citizen of the UK, you must have a
UK bank account.

☐ **B** To apply to become a permanent resident or
naturalised citizen of the UK, you must be able
to speak and read English.

Question 3   Which of the following statements is correct?

☐ **A** Women in Britain make up about a quarter of
the workforce.

☐ **B** Women in Britain make up about half of
the workforce.

Question 4   Which of the following rights did Acts of Parliament in
1870 and 1882 give married women?

Question 5   Which of the following is a traditional pub game in
the UK?

☐ **A** Scrabble
☐ **B** Pool
☐ **C** Rounders
☐ **D** Poker

Question 6   Is the statement below ☐ TRUE or ☐ FALSE?

*King Henry VIII established the Church of England
when the Pope refused to grant him a divorce.*

Question 7   Is the statement below ☐ TRUE or ☐ FALSE?

British scientists were the first to clone a mammal successfully.

Question 8   What is a bank holiday?

☐ **A** A public holiday when banks and many other businesses close for the day

☐ **B** A holiday just for people working in banks

☐ **C** A week off for everyone in the UK

☐ **D** An extra holiday entitlement for working longer hours than usual

Question 9   Is the statement below ☐ TRUE or ☐ FALSE?

There is a dragon on the official flag of Wales.

Question 10   Which country did Germany invade in 1939 that led to the UK declaring war on Germany?

☐ **A** Austria

☐ **B** Finland

☐ **C** Poland

☐ **D** France

Question 11   Which TWO of the following is William Shakespeare famous for writing?

☐ **A** Plays and TV dramas

☐ **B** Poems and radio scripts

☐ **C** Plays and poems

☐ **D** TV dramas and radio scripts

Question 12 Which of the following statements is correct?

☐ **A** Winston Churchill was the British Prime Minister during the First World War.

☐ **B** Winston Churchill was the British Prime Minister during the Second World War.

Question 13 Which TWO of the following are British overseas territories?

☐ **A** Canada and Malaysia

☐ **B** Falklands Islands and St Helena

☐ **C** Falkland Islands and Malaysia

☐ **D** Canada and St Helena

Question 14 Which of the following statements is correct?

☐ **A** After the Bill of Rights was declared in 1689, two political groups emerged, the Whigs and the Tories.

☐ **B** After the Bill of Rights was declared in 1689, two political groups emerged, the Labour Party and the Greens.

Question 15 Which UK city hosted the 2012 Paralympic Games?

☐ **A** Belfast

☐ **B** Cardiff

☐ **C** Edinburgh

☐ **D** London

Question 16 Is the statement below ☐ TRUE or ☐ FALSE?

Some people rent land called 'an allotment', where they grow fruit and vegetables.

Question 17 When walking your dog in a public place, what must you ensure?

☐ **A** That your dog wears a special dog coat

☐ **B** That your dog never strays more than 3 metres away from you

☐ **C** That your dog does not come into contact with other dogs

☐ **D** That your dog wears a collar showing the name and address of the owner

Question 18 Is the statement below ☐ TRUE or ☐ FALSE?

Wales united with England during the reign of Henry VIII.

Question 19 Which of the following statements is correct?

☐ **A** The UK is governed by the parliament sitting in Westminster.

☐ **B** The UK is governed by the parliament sitting in Edinburgh.

Question 20 What are TWO benefits of volunteering?

☐ **A** You can earn additional money and you are given a courtesy car as transport.

☐ **B** You can meet new people and you are given a courtesy car as transport.

☐ **C** You can meet new people and you help to make your community a better place.

☐ **D** You can earn additional money and you can meet new people.

Question 21 Is the statement below ☐ TRUE or ☐ FALSE?

A traditional food in Wales is Ulster fry.

Question 22 Which TWO are famous British authors?

☐ **A** Mary Quant and Henry Moore

☐ **B** Thomas Hardy and Graham Greene

☐ **C** Thomas Hardy and Henry Moore

☐ **D** Graham Greene and Henry Moore

Question 23 How are local councils funded?

☐ **A** Through money raised from local fundraising events

☐ **B** Through donations from local people

☐ **C** By central government and local taxes

☐ **D** From local businesses

Question 24 Is the statement below ☐ TRUE or ☐ FALSE?

William Blake, Lord Byron and Robert Browning were all famous golfers.

Answers to Practice Test 17

Question number	Answer	Explanation	Handbook chapter	Handbook page reference
1	FALSE	The Union Flag consists of three crosses – the crosses of St George (England), St Andrew (Scotland) and St Patrick (Ireland).	A long and illustrious history	Page 45
2	B	To apply to become a permanent resident or naturalised citizen of the UK, you must be able to speak and read English. You must also have a good understanding of life in the UK.	The values and principles of the UK	Page 9
3	B	Women in Britain make up about half of the workforce. Employment opportunities for women are much greater than they were in the past.	A modern, thriving society	Page 75
4	C	Until 1870, when a woman got married, her earnings, property and money automatically belonged to her husband. Acts of Parliament in 1870 and 1882 gave wives the right to keep their own earnings and property.	A long and illustrious history	Page 50
5	B	Pool and darts are traditional pub games. Pub quizzes are also popular.	A modern, thriving society	Page 106
6	TRUE	To divorce his first wife (Catherine of Aragon), Henry needed the approval of the Pope. When the Pope refused, Henry established the Church of England. In this new Church, the king, not the Pope, would have the power to appoint bishops and order how people should worship.	A long and illustrious history	Page 27
7	TRUE	True – The British team were the first to succeed in cloning a mammal, Dolly the sheep.	A long and illustrious history	Page 65

Question number	Answer	Explanation	Handbook chapter	Handbook page reference
8	A	There are public holidays each year, called bank holidays, when banks and many other businesses close for the day.	A modern, thriving society	Page 84
9	TRUE	Wales has its own flag, which shows a dragon. The Welsh dragon does not appear on the Union Flag because, when the first Union Flag was created in 1606 from the flags of Scotland and England, the Principality of Wales was already united with England.	A long and illustrious history	Page 46
10	C	When Adolf Hitler invaded Poland in 1939, Britain and France, declared war on Germany in order to stop his aggression.	A long and illustrious history	Page 56
11	C	William Shakespeare (1564–1616) was a playwright and actor. His plays and poems are still performed and studied in Britain and other countries today.	A long and illustrious history	Page 30
12	B	Winston Churchill was the British Prime Minister from 1940 to 1945, during the Second World War.	A long and illustrious history	Page 56
13	B	There are several British overseas territories in other parts of the world, such as St Helena and the Falkland Islands. They are linked to the UK but are not a part of it.	What is the UK?	Page 13
14	A	After the Bill of Rights was declared in 1689, there were two main groups in Parliament, known as the Whigs and the Tories. (The modern Conservative Party is still sometimes referred to as the Tories.)	A long and illustrious history	Page 37

Question number	Answer	Explanation	Handbook chapter	Handbook page reference
15	D	The Paralympic Games for 2012 were hosted in London.	A modern, thriving society	Page 84
16	TRUE	A lot of people have gardens at home and will spend their free time looking after them. Some people rent additional land called 'an allotment', where they grow fruit and vegetables.	A modern, thriving society	Page 101
17	D	All dogs in public places must wear a collar showing the name and address of the owner.	A modern, thriving society	Page 107
18	TRUE	During the reign of Henry VIII, Wales became formally united with England by the Act for the Government of Wales.	A long and illustrious history	Page 28
19	A	The UK is governed by the parliament sitting in Westminster. Scotland, Wales and Northern Ireland also have parliaments or assemblies of their own, with devolved powers in defined areas.	What is the UK?	Page 13
20	C	Volunteering is working for good causes without payment. There are many benefits to volunteering, including meeting new people and helping make your community a better place.	The UK government, the law and your role	Page 158
21	FALSE	Ulster fry is a traditional food in Northern Ireland. It is a fried meal with bacon, eggs, sausage, black pudding, white pudding, tomatoes, mushrooms, soda bread and potato bread.	A modern, thriving society	Page 102

Question number	Answer	Explanation	Handbook chapter	Handbook page reference
22	B	Thomas Hardy's best-known novels include *Far from the Madding Crowd* and *Jude the Obscure*. Graham Greene's novels include *The Heart of the Matter*, *The Honorary Consul*, *Brighton Rock* and *Our Man in Havana*.	A modern, thriving society	Page 98
23	C	Towns, cities and rural areas in the UK are governed by democratically elected councils, often called 'local authorities'. These are funded by money from central government and by local taxes.	The UK government, the law and your role	Page 129
24	FALSE	William Blake, Lord Byron and Robert Browning were all poets.	A modern, thriving society	Page 99